Lentil & Split Pea Cookbook

Edited by Merilee Frets

Peanut Butter Publishing
Seattle, Washington

Editor: Merilee Frets
Cover and Page Design: Kris Morgan
Typesetting: Grafisk

Copyright © 1990 by USA Dry Pea & Lentil Industry
All rights reserved. Printed in the United States of America
ISBN 0-89716-352-4

Published by Peanut Butter Publishing
200 Second Ave. W.
Seattle, WA 98119
(206) 281-5965

Distributed by:
Acropolis Books Ltd.
11741 Bowman Green Dr.
Reston, VA 22090

Warehouse and Customer Service:
Acropolis Books Ltd.
13950 Park Center Road
Herndon, VA 22071

TABLE OF CONTENTS

ACKNOWLEDGEMENTS

This cookbook is the result of the combined efforts of the men and women of the pea and lentil industry. The project was funded by the Washington and Idaho Dry Pea and Lentil Commissions, Moscow, Idaho.

Nutrition information contained in this cookbook was obtained with the Nutritionist III computer software program for calorie count; grams of protein, total fat, carbohydrate, and dietary fiber; and milligrams of sodium and cholesterol.

Analysis is computed for a single serving, based on the largest number of servings listed for the recipe. It *does not include* optional ingredients or those for which no specific amount is stated (salt added to taste, for example). If an ingredient is listed with an alternative — such as unflavored yogurt or sour cream — the figures are calculated using the first choice. Likewise, if a range is given for the amount of an ingredient (such as ½ to 1 cup celery), values are figured on the first, lower amount.

INTRODUCTION

Lentils and dry peas are among the oldest foods cultivated by humankind. They are grown and eaten on every continent in the world and are notable expressions of the cuisines in the Mediterranean countries of Europe and North Africa, the Near and Middle East, and Egypt. In the Old Testament, it is said the Esau traded his birthright for a "potage of lentils."

In the world market, dry peas and lentils are called "pulses" — that is, seeds that grow in pods on plants that fix nitrogen into the soil. Beans and chickpeas are also pulses, and they all are members of the legume family, which is gaining more and more recognition for its importance in supplying fiber, complex carbohydrates, protein, and essential nutrients to the diet.

Dry pea and lentil production in the United States has been centered primarily in one region of the country for about 70 years — a 250-mile long, 50-mile wide band of incredibly rich agricultural land that straddles the border of Washington and Idaho called "the Palouse." (Roughly translated, that's French for "green lawn.") Farmers in this area grow about 320 million pounds of dry peas and 135 million pounds of lentils annually in crop rotation with wheat and barley. Historically, up to 80 percent of the crops have been exported.

Peas and lentils are planted in the spring. Allowed to dry naturally on the vine in the mellow Palouse summer sun, they are harvested in late summer in a mechanical process that separates the pods from the seeds. At the processing plant, lentils are sifted and culled for uniformity in size. Seeds, field dirt, and other debris are removed by a mechanical process which uses neither water nor chemicals. Therefore, directions for cooking lentils as well as split peas state "rinse before cooking" to remove whatever remains of the fine Palouse dust.

Dry peas are processed a bit differently. After being sifted and culled for uniformity in size, they are steamed to remove the seed coat, and then put into a splitter where the peas are batted with huge paddles that cause them to split along their natural seam. The seed coats are screened off, and the split peas are again sifted and culled. Finally they are "polished" mechanically to produce a clean, uniformly-sized split pea. Dry split peas come in green and yellow varieties, with green split peas consumed more widely in the United States.

Most lentils grown in the United States are large-seeded green varieties, which appear green to tan or brown in the package. (Sunlight causes the seed coat to darken.) With American emphasis on quick-cooking products, the Red Chief lentil variety is gaining in popularity. The skin has been removed (a process known as decortication), which exposes the attractive red-orange seed that turns golden after cooking. Some fiber value, however, is lost in the decortication process.

No introduction to peas and lentils would be complete without mentioning their nutrition importance. Most of their great nutritional benefits come from their membership in the legume family. They are high in fiber, complex carbohydrates, protein, B-vitamins, and potassium; and they have just a trace of polyunsaturated fat, very low sodium, and no cholesterol.

A half-cup of cooked lentils has just 105 calories; a half-cup of split peas just 115 calories. Each half-cup contains 4 grams of dietary fiber, with 1.7 of those grams as soluble fiber (the kind that helps to reduce blood cholesterol and blood sugar). Nearly identical in nutrition composition, each half cup contains about 8 grams of protein, 20 grams of carbohydrate, and 360 milligrams of potassium.

Since they are a vegetable protein, not every essential amino acid is part of their protein make-up. Thus, lentils and split peas need to be complemented with cereals, grains, rice, nuts or seeds, or small amounts of animal proteins, such as meat or dairy products.

The American Institute for Cancer Research recommends "liberal consumption" of lentils and split peas in its dietary guidelines to lower cancer risk. In addition, the American Heart Association and the USDA both recommend *reducing* our intake of fat, sodium, and processed foods and *increasing* our intake of fresh fruits, vegetables, and high-fiber foods like lentils and split peas. And prominent members of the medical profession agree, too:

> *"Generous fiber intakes are important for good health. Fiber-rich foods, such as lentils and split peas, play a significant role in treating and preventing obesity, cardiovascular disease, hypertension and diabetes — the chronic diseases of modern man."* — Dr. James Anderson, M.D., University of Kentucky Medical School and principal investigator in several landmark studies involving the influence of diet on disease.

Lentils and split peas are healthy, versatile, easy to fix, and very, very tasty. Their mild, nutty flavor readily absorbs and harmonizes with spices and herbs, and provides an excellent complement to fish, fowl, beef, pork, and lamb — or they can be a complete meal in themselves.

You care about healthy food choices, and you care about delicious food. Welcome to the adventures of cooking with lentils and split peas. Good eating!

BASIC COOKING INSTRUCTIONS FOR LENTILS AND SPLIT PEAS

These are general guidelines for cooking. Results will vary depending on hardness of water, altitude, cooking equipment, or age of the product.

- Rinse and drain split peas or lentils
- DO NOT SOAK
- Use twice the amount of liquid as split peas or lentils
- Because it tends to toughen the seed coat and lengthen cooking time, add salt, if needed, at the end of the cooking time

In a saucepan, combine split peas or lentils and liquid. Cover; bring to a boil. Reduce heat and simmer:

15 minutes for salads
30 minutes for vegetables and main dish recipes
45 minutes for soups and purees

Drain lentils and split peas for salad recipes.
Pressure cooking is not advised.

MICROWAVE COOKING INSTRUCTIONS

- Cooking time is about the same as for stove top method
- Buzzing split peas for a minute in a food processor chops them just a little to expose more surfaces and help shorten cooking time
- Use twice the amount of liquid as split peas or lentils
- Always cover — preferably with stretch plastic wrap
- Bring to a boil on HIGH (100%) power
- Reduce heat to MEDIUM (50%) power for remainder of cooking time
- No need to check or stir as frequently as stove top

LENTIL OR SPLIT PEA PUREE

Add fiber, protein, and extra moistness to your baked goods by adding puree to the batter. Here's how to make the basic puree:

Add 2½ times the amount of water as split peas or lentils. Bring to a boil, reduce heat, cover and simmer for 45 minutes — the longer they cook, the thicker and softer they become. Stir frequently. Cool slightly and do not drain. In small batches, mash or puree lentils or split peas with a sieve, food mill, blender, food processor, or potato masher. Puree should be the consistency of canned pumpkin. Add water to thin, if needed.

Covered and refrigerated, puree should keep up to one week. It also freezes well.

One pound of split peas makes about 6 cups of puree.
One pound of lentils makes about 7 cups of puree.

LENTIL SPROUTS

There's no need to purchase lentils from a health food store. Lentils purchased from the supermarket will sprout just as well.

Place ¼ cup washed lentils in a jar. Add 2 cups lukewarm water, cover with sprouting lid, or a piece of cheesecloth secured with a jar ring or rubber band, and let stand overnight. Drain off water, turning jar upside down until *all* the water is drained out.

Hold the jar on its side and shake so the lentils are separated and spread around the sides of the jar. If you wish to have light-colored sprouts place the jar in a cupboard or closet; sprouts will be greener if left in a warm and light, but not sunny, spot.

Each morning hold the jar under the faucet and rinse sprouts well in lukewarm water. Drain carefully, shake the spouts along the side of the jar again and return to its growing spot. Seeds will sprout in 4 to 5 days.

APPETIZERS

CHEESY LENTIL DIP

1 pound lean ground beef

1 cup lentils

2½ cups water

Butter

One package taco seasoning

1 cup sour cream

½ cup green chili taco sauce

Grated cheese

Fry, crumble, and drain the hamburger. Cook the lentils in the water until they are soft. Mash, cool, and fry the lentils with a little butter.

Mix the taco seasoning with the hamburger and lentils, and spread in a 9-inch-square baking dish.

Mix together the sour cream and taco sauce. Spread over the meat and lentil mixture. Cover with grated cheese and bake in the oven at 350 degrees until the cheese melts.

Makes about 3 cups

A one-pound bag of split peas or lentils contains about 2⅓ cups.

Nutritional analysis per serving   243 calories   10.7 g carbohydrate   55.2 mg cholesterol   2.2 g dietary fiber
16.9 g protein   14.98 g fat   122.4 mg sodium

CRUNCHY INDIAN SNACK

¼ cup each (uncooked):

   Lentils

   Long grain rice

   Yellow split peas

About 3 cups water

2 tablespoons salad oil

1 tablespoon sesame seeds

1 teaspoon each:

   Ground coriander

   Ground cumin

½ teaspoon ground turmeric

½ cup each:

   Roasted and salted peanuts

   Cashews

¼ cup raisins

⅛ to ¼ teaspoon cayenne

¼ teaspoon ground cloves

1 teaspoon salt

Tortilla or potato chips, optional

Rinse the lentils, rice, and peas, and place in a pan with the water. Bring to a boil and boil for 1 minute. Remove the pan from the heat, cover, and set aside for 10 minutes. Drain and rinse the lentils, rice, and peas in cold water. Then, spread on paper towels and pat dry.

In a wide frying pan, heat the oil over medium heat. Add the lentils, rice, and peas, sesame seeds, coriander, cumin, and turmeric. Cook, stirring until toasted (10 to 15 minutes). Remove from the heat and stir in the nuts, raisins, cayenne, cloves, and salt. Store the mixture airtight for up to a week.

To serve, pour the mixture into a bowl and surround it with chips, or serve plain as finger food.

Makes about 2 cups

Nutritional analysis per serving | 278 calories | 23.19 g carbohydrate | 0 mg cholesterol | 4.101 g dietary fiber

9.079 g protein | 18.27 g fat | 367.4 mg sodium

LENTIL HUMMUS DIP

1 cup lentils, rinsed

3½ cups water

One onion, stuck with one clove

Cheese cloth bag with:

　Four sprigs parsley

　One bay leaf

　¼ teaspoon dried thyme

1½ teaspoons salt

Two cloves garlic

⅓ cup lemon juice

⅓ cup Tahini (sesame seed paste)

¼ cup olive oil

Cover the lentils with the water; add onion and cheesecloth bag. Bring to a boil, and then simmer in a covered saucepan for approximately 45 minutes or until the lentils are tender. Add the salt and simmer 5 more minutes; discard the onion and cheesecloth bag, and drain. With the motor running on your food processor, mince the garlic cloves. Add and blend the lentils in batches, alternating with the Tahini. Add the oil in a stream and blend until smooth. Add the lemon juice.

Transfer the dip to a ceramic bowl and cover with a thin layer of olive oil. Sprinkle with fresh parsley or cilantro.

Makes 3 cups

Serve as a dip with pita bread or first course on thick slices of chicken, ribs, or lamb chops from grill, or fresh vegetables.

Nutritional analysis per serving　　　141 calories　　　11.92 g carbohydrate　　　0 mg cholesterol　　　3.155 g dietary fiber
　　　　　　　　　　　　　　　　　4.882 g protein　　　8.989 g fat　　　415.6 mg sodium

LENTIL SPREAD

1 cup lentils, rinsed

½ cup white rice

3 tablespoons chopped dry onion

1 teaspoon chopped garlic

1 teaspoon ground oregano

One bay leaf

4 cups water

Two apples (we suggest Granny Smiths), peeled, grated, and mixed with the juice of ½ lemon

2 teaspoons sweet hot mustard

⅛ teaspoon pepper

1 teaspoon curry powder

Put in a saucepan the lentils, rice, onion, garlic, oregano, and bay leaf. Add the water, bring to a boil, and then simmer for 45 minutes. When the rice and lentils are tender, drain, remove the bay leaf, and blend in a blender or food processor until smooth. Add the grated apples, mustard, pepper, and curry powder. Chill in a covered jar.

Serve this spread on bread, crackers, or toast.

Makes about 3 cups

Lentils grow in pods like peas, but the pods are smaller and there are only one or two seeds in each pod.

Nutritional analysis per serving   130 calories   27.11 g carbohydrate   0 mg cholesterol   4.598 g dietary fiber
6.344 g protein   0.342 g fat   45.4 mg sodium

Nachos

1 cup lentils, rinsed

½ pound lean ground beef, salted and peppered to taste

One can (8 ounces) tomato sauce

1 teaspoon chili powder

1 teaspoon Tabasco sauce

½ cup picante or salsa sauce

1 cup water

Two or three green onions, chopped

½ cup chopped ripe olives

Two or three green chili peppers, chopped

½ cup shredded cheddar cheese

½ cup shredded Monterey Jack or mozzarella cheese

Nacho chips

Sour cream, guacamole, additional olives, and chopped tomatoes for the garnish, to taste

Cook the lentils in 2 cups of water for approximately 30 minutes; drain. In a large frying pan, brown the ground beef with salt and pepper, to taste. Spoon off the excess fat. Add the tomato sauce, chili powder, Tabasco sauce, picante or salsa, and the 1 cup of water. Stir over medium heat until slightly thickened; stir in the drained lentils. Place in a 9-inch pie pan or an 8-inch-square baking dish. Top with the green onions, chopped olives, green chilies, and shredded cheeses. Heat in a 350-degree oven for 10 to 12 minutes, or microwave until the cheese melts. Garnish and serve with chips for dipping.

Serves 8

| Nutritional analysis per serving | 195 calories | 13.58 g carbohydrate | 34.45 mg cholesterol | 3.096 g dietary fiber |
| | 14.14 g protein | 10.11 g fat | 370.4 mg sodium | |

6

PEA-CHEDDAR DIP

½ cup yellow split peas, rinsed*

2 cups water

2 cups grated cheddar cheese

Half a small onion, finely minced

Salt and pepper, to taste

Combine the split peas with 2 cups of water. Bring rapidly to a boil and then reduce the heat to simmer. Cover tightly and cook gently for 45 to 50 minutes until the peas are very tender. The hardness of water and height of altitude influences the cooking time.

Place the cooked and drained peas in a blender with the cheddar cheese, the onion, salt, and pepper. Blend until smooth. Serve this dip hot as a vegetable sauce or fondue, or cold as a dip for chips or a spread for little sandwiches or celery.

* Use green split peas to make a green dip.

Makes about 2½ cups

Remember . . . don't soak . . . don't soak . . . don't soak.

Nutritional analysis per serving	195 calories	8.458 g carbohydrate	39.67 mg cholesterol	0.22 g dietary fiber
	12.19 g protein	12.7 g fat	235.3 mg sodium	

RED LENTIL PATE

2 cups Red Chief lentils*

3½ cups water

One large onion

2 tablespoons vegetable oil

1½ teaspoons chopped garlic

1 teaspoon each:

   Dried basil

   Thyme

   Cumin

¼ cup bread crumbs

1½ tablespoons dried parsley

1 teaspoon salt

½ teaspoon pepper

1 teaspoon tarragon vinegar

Wash the lentils quickly, drain, and place in a 3- to 4-quart saucepan. Add the water, bring to a boil, reduce the heat to medium, and simmer, covered, for 20 minutes.

Chop the onion. In a large skillet, heat the oil. Add the garlic, onion, and herbs, and saute over medium heat, stirring constantly, for about 10 minutes, or until the onion and garlic is browned and fragrant.

Oil a 9-inch shallow baking pan or loaf pan and sprinkle with half of the bread crumbs, completely coating the inside of the pan. Preheat the oven to 375 degrees. Chop the parsley finely.

When the lentils are done, stir them thoroughly to mash, add the onion mixture, bread crumbs, and parsley. Season to taste with salt, pepper, vinegar. Pour the lentil mixture into the pan and bake for 20 to 30 minutes, or until set. Allow to cool at room temperature before slicing.

Serves 8

* Red Chief lentils are available at health food stores. Or, substitute regular lentils and adjust the cooking time accordingly.

Nutritional analysis per serving	144 calories	21.4 g carbohydrate	0 mg cholesterol	4.65 g dietary fiber
	7.794 g protein	3.705 g fat	317.6 mg sodium	

SPLIT PEA DIP

One onion, chopped

3 tablespoons oil, divided

3½ cups water

1 cup green split peas, rinsed

¼ cup finely chopped green chilies

Two cloves garlic, minced

Juice of one lemon

Two tomatoes, peeled, seeded, and chopped

2 tablespoons chopped, fresh cilantro leaves

½ teaspoon cumin

Few drops Chinese chili oil

Salt

Saute the onion in 2 tablespoons of oil in a 1½- to 2-quart saucepan until tender but not browned. Stir in the water and split peas. Bring to a boil. Boil for 2 minutes, remove from the heat, cover, and let stand for 30 minutes.

Place the pan over the heat again and bring to a boil. Cover, reduce the heat and let the mixture simmer for about 20 minutes or until the peas are tender. Cool slightly, and then drain the peas, reserving any liquid. Puree the peas in a food processor or blender, adding enough of the reserved liquid to reach the desired dipping consistency.

Place the pureed peas in a bowl and stir in the chilies, garlic, lemon juice, tomatoes, cilantro, cumin, and remaining oil. Season the mixture to taste with a few drops of chili oil and salt. Cover and chill well.

Makes about 3 cups

Nutritional analysis per serving   165 calories   20.35 g carbohydrate   0 mg cholesterol   1.093 g dietary fiber
     6.279 g protein   7.547 g fat   48.28 mg sodium

TEXAS LENTIL DIP

1 cup lentils, washed and drained

2 cups water

¼ cup mayonnaise

¼ cup sour cream

1 teaspoon dry mustard

1 teaspoon red pepper

Salt, if needed

Combine the lentils and water in a saucepan. Bring to a boil; reduce the heat, cover, and simmer for 40 minutes, or until soft. Drain and mash the lentils. Combine with the remaining ingredients and mix well.

Serve with tortilla chips.

Serves 8

Dry split peas come in two colors — green and yellow. Lentils, however, come in many shapes and colors, often depending on the country from which they come. The U.S. and Canada grow mostly large-seeded green varieties, which look tan or brown in the store. France grows a small-seeded green variety that looks almost black. Egypt, Turkey, and India grow a small-seeded red lentil that is often skinned (decorticated), split, and brilliant orange in color.

Nutritional analysis per serving	120 calories	10.53 g carbohydrate	7.188 mg cholesterol	2.45 g dietary fiber
	4.45 g protein	7.16 g fat	58.19 mg sodium	

SOUPS & STEWS

Excellent

LENTIL BARLEY SOUP

1 cup chopped onion

1 cup chopped celery

1 clove garlic, minced

¼ cup vegetable oil

1 can (28 ounces) tomatoes or 4 cups diced fresh tomatoes

¾ cup lentils, rinsed

¾ cup pearl barley

6 cups water

6 vegetarian bouillon cubes

½ teaspoon dried rosemary, crushed

½ teaspoon dried oregano, crushed

¼ teaspoon pepper

2 cups thinly sliced carrots

1 cup shredded Swiss cheese, optional

In a large, heavy soup pot, cook the onions, celery, and garlic in hot oil until tender. Add the water, tomatoes, lentils, barley, bouillon cubes, rosemary, oregano, pepper, and carrots. Cook for 40 minutes, or until the barley, lentils, and carrots are tender. Top with Swiss cheese, if desired.

Serves 10

Lentil and split pea soups are great to make ahead, because they hold well in the refrigerator or freezer. They will thicken as they keep, so if you prefer a more diluted soup, just stir in additional water or broth while the soup is reheating.

Nutritional analysis per serving	170 calories	25.72 g carbohydrate	0.086 mg cholesterol	5.659 g dietary fiber
	5.284 g protein	6.007 g fat	683.1 mg sodium	

BACK-AT-THE-RANCH
CARROT SOUP

4 cups coarsely grated carrots

1½ cups chopped onions

1 tablespoon minced garlic

2½ tablespoons vegetable oil

1 pound lentils, rinsed

3 quarts water

2½ tablespoons lemon juice

½ teaspoon dried thyme

Salt to taste

⅛ teaspoon cayenne pepper

1 cup unseasoned croutons

Saute the carrots, onion, and garlic in the vegetable oil until the vegetables are soft, for about 5 minutes. Stir in the lentils and saute for 1 minute. Add the water, bring to a boil, and reduce to a simmer. Cook, uncovered, over medium heat until the lentils are very soft and the soup is thickened, for about 45 minutes. Stir in the lemon juice, thyme, salt, and pepper.

Serve this soup garnished with croutons.

Serves 8

Nutritional analysis per serving   179 calories   27.9 g carbohydrate   0 mg cholesterol   7.169 g dietary fiber
8.966 g protein   4.451 g fat   49.99 mg sodium

BASIC
CREAM OF LENTIL SOUP

2 cups lentils, rinsed

1 quart chicken stock

1 quart water

Two medium onions, chopped

Two medium potatoes, chopped

3 tablespoons butter or margarine

2 tablespoons flour

2 cups milk, whole

Salt and pepper, to taste

Sour cream and grated lemon rind, for garnish

Cook together in a Dutch oven or stock pot, the lentils, chicken stock, water, and vegetables for about 45 minutes. When cooked, blend thoroughly until smooth.

Make a white sauce with the butter and flour. Add the sauce to the soup pot and simmer for 5 minutes. Add the milk, salt, and pepper. Top the soup with a little sour cream and sprinkle with grated lemon.

Serves 12

Nutritional analysis per serving   160 calories   23.12 g carbohydrate   8.583 mg cholesterol   3.88 g dietary fiber
9.751 g protein   3.595 g fat   322.2 mg sodium

Black Forest
Split Pea Soup

2 tablespoons margarine

Two medium onions, finely
chopped

Two medium carrots, diced

One celery stalk, thinly sliced

1⅔ cups green split peas, rinsed

One medium potato, diced

One ham hock or one meaty ham
bone

One bottle or can of beer (12 ounces)

6 cups water, or more if needed

1 teaspoon dried thyme

1 teaspoon whole mustard seed,
crushed

⅛ teaspoon ground cloves

½ pound veal frankfurters, sliced
½-inch-thick

2 tablespoons cider vinegar

Salt, to taste, optional

¼ cup each:

Chopped parsley

Sliced green onions

Melt the margarine in a large kettle,
add the onions, carrots, and celery, and
cook with the split peas. When the vegetables are soft but not browned, add
the potatoes, ham hock, beer, water,
and seasonings. Simmer until the peas
are very tender, for 1 to 2 hours, stirring occasionally.

Remove the ham hock. When cool,
return the meat to the soup in large
chunks. Add the frankfurter slices and
reheat the soup to serving temperature.
Blend in the vinegar. Salt if needed. Stir
in the parsley and green onions.

Serves 6

Nutritional analysis per serving   333 calories   36.21 g carbohydrate   21.73 mg cholesterol   2.248 g dietary fiber
   14.54 g protein   13.84 g fat   504 mg sodium

BOUQUET GARNI FRENCH MARKET SOUP

1 cup yellow split peas, rinsed

1 cup navy beans, presoaked overnight

Bouquet garni bag:*

    Fresh parsley sprigs or 1 tablespoon dried parsley

    One bay leaf, crushed

    1/3 teaspoon thyme

    1/3 teaspoon marjoram

    Two garlic cloves, crushed

    1/4 cup minced, fresh celery leaves

    1 teaspoon dried chives

2 cups fresh or canned tomatoes, chunked

8 ounces tomato sauce

Four celery stalks, chopped

Two onions, chopped

Salt and pepper, to taste

Two cooked, boneless chicken breasts, chunked into bite-sized pieces

1½ cups red wine, added just before serving

½ cup chopped, fresh or dried parsley, for garnish

Add 2 quarts of water to the peas and beans, and simmer, covered, with the bouquet garni bag until the navy beans are tender, for about 2 hours. Remove the bouquet garni bag.

Add the remaining ingredients and simmer for about 30 minutes. Serve hot but, just before serving, add the red wine and parsley.

* Any combination of herbs may be used. Gather the herbs in a 6-inch square of cheesecloth, tie with a white thread, and float in a kettle. (Do not use members of the cabbage family; they taste like sulfur after long cooking. And avoid oregano and dill because they become bitter if simmered long.)

Serves 8 to 10

Nutritional analysis per serving   248 calories   25.47 g carbohydrate   79.54 mg cholesterol   3.684 g dietary fiber
     31.11 g protein   19.78 g fat   881.8 mg sodium

BROWN RICE AND LENTIL STEW

¾ cup brown rice

½ cup lentils, rinsed

2 cups water

½ cup chopped onions

½ cup sliced celery

½ cup sliced carrots

¼ cup snipped, fresh parsley

1 teaspoon Italian seasoning

One garlic clove, minced

One bay leaf

2½ cups chicken broth

One can (14½ ounces) peeled, whole tomatoes, undrained and chopped

1 tablespoon cider vinegar

Combine all the ingredients in a Dutch oven or large saucepan; bring to a boil. Reduce the heat and simmer, uncovered, stirring occasionally, for 55 minutes to 1 hour, or until the rice is tender. Remove the bay leaf.

Serves 4

Add split peas or lentils to any favorite soup or stew recipe. The benefits? More complex carbohydrates, more fiber, less fat, less sodium, and less cholesterol than other protein ingredients.

Nutritional analysis per serving	246.6 calories	47.2 g carbohydrate	0.625 mg cholesterol	6.342 g dietary fiber
	11.5 g protein	1.982 g fat	685 mg sodium	

Chili con Lentils

1 pound lentils, rinsed

5 cups water

One can (16 ounces) tomatoes or tomato sauce

½ cup chopped onion

2 teaspoons chili powder

1 teaspoon salt

½ teaspoon cumin

2 tablespoons dried parsley flakes

Combine the lentils and water in a large saucepan. Bring to a boil; reduce the heat, cover, and simmer for 30 minutes. Do not drain. Add the tomatoes, onion, chili powder, salt, cumin, and parsley flakes. Simmer for 30 minutes more. Adjust the consistency of the soup with water, if needed.

Makes 7 cups

Nutritional analysis per serving	160.8 calories	30.34 g carbohydrate	0 mg cholesterol	7.518 g dietary fiber
	11.6 g protein	0.366 g fat	464.8 mg sodium	

Easy Meatless Lentil Chili

1 pound lentils, rinsed

5 cups water

One can (16 ounces) tomatoes or tomato sauce

One package dry onion soup mix

1½ teaspoons chili powder

½ teaspoon cumin

Combine the lentils and water in a large saucepan and simmer for 30 minutes; do not drain. Add the tomatoes, soup mix, chili powder, and cumin. Simmer for 30 minutes more.

Serves 6

Nutritional analysis per serving	209.6 calories	40.07 g carbohydrate	0.333 mg cholesterol	9.426 g dietary fiber
	14.37 g protein	0.674 g fat	1129 mg sodium	

CHILI DELUXE

5 cups water

One can (16 ounces) chickpeas, drained

1 cup chopped onion

½ cup chopped celery

One large garlic clove, minced

2 teaspoons ground cumin

1 teaspoon salt

1 pound lentils, rinsed

One can (16 ounces) kidney beans, drained

One can (16 ounces) tomatoes, cut up, or substitute fresh tomatoes

½ cup chopped carrots

½ cup chopped green peppers

1 tablespoon chili powder

1 teaspoon crushed red pepper flakes

Cheddar cheese for topping

In a large, heavy pan, combine all the ingredients. Cover; bring to a boil. Reduce the heat and simmer for 30 minutes, or until the lentils are tender. Top the chili with shredded cheddar cheese.

Serves 10 to 12

Cumin seed has a slightly bitter flavor and odor.

Nutritional analysis per serving	295 calories	54.47 g carbohydrate	0 mg cholesterol	14.25 g dietary fiber
	18.79 g protein	1.991 g fat	919.3 mg sodium	

Excellent

CLASSIC AMERICAN
SPLIT PEA SOUP

1 cup green or yellow split peas, rinsed

4 cups ham or chicken stock

⅓ cup chopped onion

⅓ cup chopped celery

⅓ cup diced carrots

One medium potato, peeled and diced

One bay leaf

1 cup diced, cooked ham

Salt and pepper to taste

Combine all the ingredients in a large soup pot. Bring to a boil. Reduce the heat to low, cover, and simmer, stirring occasionally, until the vegetables are tender and the soup thickens, about 45 minutes to an hour. Add the salt and pepper at the end of cooking.

Makes 4 to 5 cups

Did you know . . . National Split Pea Soup Week is always the second week of November? Plan to celebrate with your favorite split pea soup recipe!

Nutritional analysis per serving	192 calories	24.11 g carbohydrate	21.6 mg cholesterol	0.81 g dietary fiber
	14.68 g protein	4.486 g fat	255 mg sodium	

EAST INDIAN
SPLIT PEA SOUP

2 cups yellow or green split peas, rinsed

8 cups water

2 tablespoons vegetable oil

One large onion, chopped

Four garlic cloves, minced

1 tablespoon minced, fresh ginger root

½ teaspoon ground cumin

¼ teaspoon coriander

½ teaspoon turmeric

⅛ teaspoon cayenne pepper

½ teaspoon curry powder, optional

1½ cups fresh spinach, chopped

Salt, to taste

Place the peas and water in a large kettle. Bring to a boil and simmer over low heat, stirring occasionally, until the peas are soft, usually for about 30 minutes. Heat the oil in a pan and saute the onion, garlic, ginger, and spices until tender. Add this mixture to the peas and continue to simmer. Add the spinach and salt during the last minutes of cooking before serving.

Serves 6

Yes, you can cook lentils and split peas in the microwave, but the cooking time will not be significantly reduced.

Nutritional analysis per serving	210 calories	31.37 g carbohydrate	0 mg cholesterol	0.805 g dietary fiber
	11.57 g protein	5.397 g fat	18.19 mg sodium	

DUMPLINGS AND LENTIL BEEF SOUP (JUST LIKE MOM'S)

2 pounds beef shanks or beef stew meat

One onion, chopped

5 quarts water

1 teaspoon salt

1 teaspoon pepper

One package (1 pound) lentils, rinsed

Three carrots, sliced

Three celery stalks, chopped

One garlic clove, minced

½ cup chopped parsley

1 tablespoon Worcestershire sauce

Grated Parmesan cheese

Parsley sprigs

DUMPLINGS

1½ cups white flour

2 teaspoons baking powder

½ teaspoon salt

3 tablespoons vegetable margarine

¾ cup milk

Place the beef shanks in a large kettle. Add the onion, 4 quarts of the water, salt, and pepper. Bring to a boil and skim. Reduce the heat, cover, and simmer for 2 hours.

When the shanks are tender, lift from the pan and remove the meat from the bones. Return the meat in serving-sized pieces to the broth. Add the lentils, carrots, celery, garlic, parsley, and Worcestershire sauce, along with 1 more quart of water. Simmer for 1 hour.

For the dumplings: Sift the dry ingredients together, cut in the margarine, and stir in the milk until the dough is blended. Drop by spoonfuls onto the boiling stew meat. Cook for 10 minutes with the kettle lid off and then 10 minutes with the lid on. Serve hot, immediately, topped with grated Parmesan cheese and parsley sprigs — with the light-as-a-feather dumplings.

Serves 6 to 8

Nutritional analysis per serving	616 calories	50.36 g carbohydrate	127 mg cholesterol	8.196 g dietary fiber
	52.3 g protein	22.19 g fat	646.3 mg sodium	

MOUNT SPOKANE LENTIL STEW

2 cups lentils, rinsed

2 cups chopped ham

Five carrots, sliced

One onion, chopped

One garlic clove

Two bay leaves

One can tomato soup

One can (16 ounces) tomatoes

2 teaspoons pepper

2½ cups water

Combine all the ingredients in a crock-pot and cook for 8 to 10 hours on medium or low heat. Remove bay leaves before serving.

Serves 10

Nutritional analysis per serving | 245.5 calories | 25.77 g carbohydrate | 32.40 g cholesterol | 5.867 g dietary fiber
5.867 g protein | 9.873 g fat | 1222 mg sodium

GERMAN LENTIL SOUP

Four bacon slices, cut up

1 cup chopped onions

1 cup sliced carrots

½ cup chopped celery

1 pound lentils, rinsed

8 cups water

2 tablespoons vinegar

1 tablespoon beef stock base or two beef bouillon cubes

2 teaspoons dry mustard

½ pound skinless frankfurters, sliced

¼ cup catsup

Salt and pepper to taste

In a Dutch oven, cook the bacon until it is fairly crisp. Add the onion, carrots, and celery; cook until the onion is transparent. Add the lentils, water, vinegar, beef stock base, and mustard. Bring to a boil. Cover, reduce the heat, and simmer for 1 hour. Add the franks, catsup, salt, and pepper, and simmer for 15 minutes.

Serves 8

For a heavy soup, it is important when stirring to reach down into the pot with the spoon to bring up the ingredients from the bottom to prevent scorching or burning on the bottom.

Nutritional analysis per serving	279 calories	25.39 g carbohydrate	24.42 mg cholesterol	5.619 g dietary fiber
	14.19 g protein	14.09 g fat	648 mg sodium	

GREEN HERB SPLIT PEA SOUP

1 pound green or yellow split peas, rinsed

4½ cups water

2 ounces low-sodium chicken base

½ cup chopped onions

3 tablespoons lemon juice

¼ teaspoon nutmeg

¼ teaspoon thyme

¼ teaspoon marjoram

1½ teaspoons sugar

⅛ teaspoon pepper

¼ teaspoon cayenne or dried, flaked hot peppers

¼ teaspoon salt

5 ounces chopped, fresh or frozen spinach

1 tablespoon dried parsley flakes

1 cup grated carrots

Place the first 11 ingredients in a 2-quart saucepan. Cook slowly until the peas are soft, for approximately 45 minutes. Whisk or blend the peas until pureed. Ten minutes before serving, add the salt, spinach, parsley, and grated carrot.

Adjust the soup's consistency with water, if needed.

Serves 8

Nutritional analysis per serving   116 calories   21.35 g carbohydrate   0.031 mg cholesterol   0.941 g dietary fiber
                                    7.940 g protein   0.632 g fat   112.2 mg sodium

HAMBURGER-VEGETABLE LENTIL SOUP

1 pound hamburger

5¾ cups tomato juice

4 cups water

1 cup lentils, rinsed

1 cup carrots, diced

1 cup cabbage, diced

1 cup celery, chopped

½ cup onions, chopped

1 teaspoon salt

½ teaspoon pepper

1 teaspoon green pepper (or green pepper flakes)

One bay leaf

Brown the hamburger until it is crumbly. Drain off the excess fat. Bring the water to a boil and add all the ingredients, including the hamburger. Again, bring the soup to a boil, reduce the heat, and simmer for about 1½ hours.

This soup freezes well.

Serves 6

*Sunlight causes lentils to darken and split peas to lighten in color.
Their nutritional value is unaffected.*

Nutritional analysis per serving	359 calories	26.82 g carbohydrate	66.71 mg cholesterol	7.406 g dietary fiber
	25.82 g protein	17.33 g fat	1294 mg sodium	

HEARTY VEGETARIAN STEW

2 tablespoons vegetable oil

1 cup chopped onions

7 cups water

Two vegetarian-style bouillon cubes or 2 teaspoons instant broth granules

1 cup lentils, rinsed

½ cup small elbow macaroni

Two medium carrots, sliced

One can (16 ounces) chickpeas, drained

½ teaspoon dried thyme leaves

Heat the vegetable oil in a 3-quart saucepan or Dutch oven. Add the onion and cook over medium-high heat, stirring often, for about 4 minutes until the onion is well-browned. Add the water, bouillon cubes, and lentils. Reduce the heat, cover, and simmer for 30 minutes. Add the remaining ingredients, cover, and simmer for 15 to 20 minutes until the lentils and carrots are tender.

Serves 8

Bouquet garni or sachet d' epice is a cheesecloth bag containing herbs and spices removed from a soup after cooking is completed. Straining the soup to remove herbs and spices accomplishes the same result.

Nutritional analysis per serving	146 calories	21.24 g carbohydrate	0.036 mg cholesterol	5.07 g dietary fiber
	5.779 g protein	4.67 g fat	454.5 mg sodium	

HIGH-ENERGY BURGER SOUP

2⅓ cups lentils

2½ quarts water

2½ cups tomatoes, chopped

One can (8 ounces) tomato sauce

One large onion, chopped

3 tablespoons fresh dill or parsley, snipped

Three garlic cloves, minced

Two bay leaves

1 pound lean ground beef

1½ teaspoons seasoned salt

¼ teaspoon pepper

One egg, slightly beaten

1 cup elbow macaroni

Rinse the lentils and combine with the water, tomatoes, tomato sauce, onion, dill or parsley, garlic, and bay leaves. Bring to a boil; reduce the heat and simmer for 30 minutes.

Meanwhile, combine the beef with the salt, pepper, and egg. Form the meat into 24 balls. Brown the meatballs in a microwave or cook in boiling water, draining off the water when the meat is cooked.

Add the meatballs and macaroni to the soup, and cook until the macaroni is tender.

Serve hot, sprinkled with Parmesan cheese, if desired.

Serves 6

A leaf of lettuce placed in a pot of soup absorbs the fat from the top.

Nutritional analysis per serving	465 calories	43.28 g carbohydrate	102.2 mg cholesterol	9.393 g dietary fiber
	33.64 g protein	18.33 g fat	726.3 mg sodium	

HUNGARIAN-STYLE LENTIL STEW

2 cups coarsely chopped onion

1/4 cup vegetable oil

1 pound mushrooms, quartered

3 tablespoons paprika

1 tablespoon caraway seeds

1/8 teaspoon cayenne, or to taste

2 cups chicken stock, canned broth, or water

1 1/2 cups lentils, rinsed

One can (14 ounces) plum tomatoes, chopped, including the juice

Two green bell peppers, chopped

1/2 cup sour cream

1 tablespoon fresh lemon juice

Salt and black pepper to taste

Buttered egg noodles, as an accompaniment if desired

In a skillet, cook the onion in the oil over moderately low heat, stirring occasionally until the onion softens. Add the mushrooms and cook until almost all of the liquid that the mushrooms give off evaporates.

Transfer the mixture to a saucepan and add the paprika, caraway seeds, cayenne, stock, 2 1/2 cups of water, and lentils. Bring the stew to a boil and simmer uncovered, for 10 minutes, or until the lentils are barely tender. Add the tomatoes and bell peppers to the stew, and simmer, stirring occasionally, for 10 minutes.

In a food processor or blender, puree 1 cup of the solids with the sour cream.

Stir the puree, lemon juice, salt, and black pepper into the stew. Serve the stew over noodles, if desired.

Serves 6

Nutritional analysis per serving | 303 calories | 34.99 g carbohydrate | 0.333 mg cholesterol | 7.727 g dietary fiber
14.07 g protein | 14.11 g fat | 428.1 mg sodium

IDAHO LENTIL BEAN POT

1 cup lentils, rinsed

One onion, chopped

Three garlic cloves, minced

One green pepper, chopped

6 ounces Italian turkey sausage, crumbled

One can (15 ounces) pinto beans, undrained

One can (15 ounces) garbanzo beans, undrained

6 ounces barbecue sauce

8 ounces tomato sauce

½ teaspoon chili powder

1 teaspoon thyme, crushed

1 teaspoon Italian seasoning

Cook the lentils in 2½ cups of water for 30 minutes. Do not drain. Combine the onion, garlic, green pepper, and sausage in a covered dish and microwave for 2 to 3 minutes or until the sausage is cooked. Drain the fat.

Combine the lentils, pinto beans, garbanzo beans, sausage mixture, and remaining ingredients in a crockpot. Cook on high for 2 hours.

Serves 4

Salt toughens the seed coat of all legumes if added at the start of the cooking time. Add, if needed, to cooked and drained lentils or split peas.

Nutritional analysis per serving   448 calories   72.24 g carbohydrate   0 mg cholesterol   18.42 g dietary fiber
30.47 g protein   5.767 g fat   2024 mg sodium

Italian Fresh-Garden Pea Soup

1½ cups yellow or green split peas, rinsed

½ cup dried navy beans, presoaked overnight

Two cans (12 ounces each) tomato juice

½ cup chopped onions

½ cup diced celery

1 cup cubed zucchini

2 cups coarsely chopped cabbage

1 cup diced turnips

1 cup diced carrots

One garlic clove, minced

1 teaspoon salt, or to taste

½ teaspoon pepper

¾ teaspoon Italian seasoning

2 ounces spaghetti, uncooked and broken in quarters

8 tablespoons Parmesan cheese

Fill a saucepan with 8 cups of water and add the split peas and navy beans. Bring to a boil; reduce the heat, cover, and simmer for 1 hour or until the beans are tender. Add the remaining ingredients to the pan except for the spaghetti and cheese. Cook until the vegetables are tender. Add the spaghetti and cook an additional 8 to 10 minutes until the spaghetti is tender. Sprinkle with cheese before serving.

Serves 8

Nutritional analysis per serving	188 calories	31.35 g carbohydrate	4.938 mg cholesterol	3.967 g dietary fiber
	12.39 g protein	2.61 g fat	735.4 mg sodium	

LENTIL-BRATWURST STEW

4 cups water

1 teaspoon dried thyme, crushed

3 cups tomato juice

½ teaspoon dried rosemary,
crushed

1½ cups lentils, rinsed

¼ teaspoon garlic powder

¼ teaspoon pepper

1 cup beer

One medium carrot, chopped

One bay leaf

12 ounces smoked bratwurst, sliced

Two medium sweet potatoes,
peeled and cut into ½-inch cubes

In a 4-quart Dutch oven, combine the first 10 ingredients. Bring to boiling; reduce the heat and simmer, covered, for 15 minutes. Stir in the bratwurst and sweet potatoes. Return to boiling; reduce the heat and simmer, covered, for 10 minutes. Remove the bay leaf.

Place half of the stew (about 6 cups) in a 1½- or 2-quart freezer container. Cool. Seal, label, and freeze. Simmer the remaining stew for 10 to 15 minutes more or until the lentils and potatoes are tender. Serve immediately.

Serves 8 (total)

Nutritional analysis per serving   269 calories   28.46 g carbohydrate   25.52 mg cholesterol   5.854 g dietary fiber
                                    13.41 g protein   11.15 g fat   597.6 mg sodium

LENTIL AND GREENS SOUP

One package (1 pound) lentils, rinsed

2 tablespoons vegetable oil

One large onion, chopped fine

Two celery stalks, chopped fine

Salt and cayenne pepper, to taste

One bay leaf

Water and/or chicken stock

One package frozen, chopped spinach or 4 cups fresh spinach or chard leaves, chopped

In a large soup pot, heat the oil; add the onion and celery, and saute until the onion is limp and translucent. Add the lentils and the rest of the ingredients, except for the greens. Add water to cover by about 2 inches.

Simmer the soup gently until the lentils are soft, usually for 40 minutes. Remove the bay leaf.

Add the greens to the soup and cook about 10 more minutes. Like most soups, this one is better the next day.

Serves 6

Acidic ingredients tend to slow the cooking of peas and lentils, so add tomatoes, for example, toward the end of the cooking time.

Nutritional analysis per serving — 299 calories, 18.3 g protein — 44.5 g carbohydrate, 7.155 g fat — 0 mg cholesterol, 106.8 mg sodium — 12.33 g dietary fiber

LENTIL-PUMPKIN ALMONDINE SOUP

½ cup blanched, slivered almonds

2 tablespoons butter

1 cup chopped onion

½ cup chopped celery

1 teaspoon curry powder

One can (16 ounces) solid-packed pumpkin

2 cups chicken broth, optional

2 cups water

½ cup lentils, rinsed

1 tablespoon lemon juice

1 cup low-fat milk

1 tablespoon honey

½ cup plain, low-fat yogurt

Spread the almonds in a single layer on a microwave-safe plate. Microwave* the almonds on high for 3 minutes, stirring and checking to prevent scorching. Cool the almonds on the counter. Remove ⅓ cup of the toasted almonds and chop finely in a food processor or blender. Set aside.

Melt the butter on high power for 1 minute in a large microwave-safe bowl. Stir in the onion, celery, and curry powder. Cover the bowl with waxed paper and microwave** on high power for 5 minutes. Remove from the oven; stir in the pumpkin, chicken broth, water, lentils, and lemon juice. Cover the bowl with waxed paper and microwave on high power for 20 minutes, stirring the soup every 5 minutes.

Remove the soup from the oven and stir in the chopped almonds, milk, and honey. Ladle the soup into serving bowls. Just before serving, dollop each bowl with 2 tablespoons of yogurt and sprinkle with the reserved almonds.

* To toast the almonds in the oven, spread the almonds in a single layer on a baking sheet. Bake at 350 degrees for 9 to 11 minutes, stirring occasionally, until the almonds are golden brown. Cool.

** This soup may be cooked on the stove — increase the water to 3 cups; simmer for 25 minutes, stirring often.

Serves 6

Never use a cooking wine in a soup recipe, as a cooking wine is too salty, strong, sour, and will overpower the flavor. Use any of your favorite table wines.

Nutritional analysis per serving	296 calories	32.59 g carbohydrate	2.203 mg cholesterol	4.624 g dietary fiber
	12.54 g protein	14.74 g fat	476 mg sodium	

LENTIL GAZPACHO

1 cup lentil puree

1½ cups fresh tomatoes, chopped

½ cup onions, chopped

One green pepper, chopped

½ cup fresh cucumber, chopped

One small green chile, chopped

Two garlic cloves, diced

48 ounces tomato juice

¼ cup lime or lemon juice, fresh

¼ teaspoon paprika

1 teaspoon dill seed

½ teaspoon basil

Salt, to taste

To make the lentil puree: In small batches, puree well-cooked lentils with reserved cooking water in a blender, adding water to thin if needed. Puree the lentils to the consistency of canned pumpkin. (Please see page *xi* for complete instructions.)

Blend the solid ingredients thoroughly in a blender. In a large bowl, mix with the lentil puree and tomato juice. Add the lemon or lime juice and spices.

Chill the soup for several hours before serving. Garnish with a twist of lemon or lime.

Serves 10

Lentils can be an important source of iron. Eating lentils with foods high in Vitamin C, such as tomatoes, green pepper, broccoli, or citrus fruits or juices helps the body absorb the iron more effectively.

Nutritional analysis per serving   58 calories   12.97 g carbohydrate   0 mg cholesterol   3.262 g dietary fiber
                                     3.185 g protein   0.235 g fat   539.5 mg sodium

Lentil Soup with Cilantro

1 cup lentils, rinsed

6 cups water

2 tablespoons olive oil

½ cup each:

    Diced onion

    Celery

    Bell pepper

2 tablespoons minced, fresh cilantro

One large garlic clove, pressed

½ teaspoon dried oregano

2 tablespoons red wine vinegar

1 teaspoon Beau Monde seasoning

Sprinkle cayenne pepper

Parmesan cheese, grated

Combine the lentils with the water in a soup pot. Bring to a boil, reduce the heat and simmer, covered, for about 30 minutes, until the lentils are tender but still retain their shape.

Meanwhile, heat the oil in a saucepan and saute the onion, celery, and pepper for 3 to 4 minutes. Add the cilantro, garlic, and oregano, and continue to saute until the vegetables are tender.

Stir the vegetables and spices into the lentils with the vinegar, Beau Monde, and cayenne pepper. Simmer for 15 minutes and serve, topped with Parmesan cheese.

Serves 4

Coriander seed has a sweet and tart lemon-like flavor. Also, when fresh, coriander is called cilantro or Mexican parsley. Use only the leaves of fresh cilantro, as the stems are bitter.

Nutritional analysis per serving	177 calories	22.77 g carbohydrate	0 mg cholesterol	5.669 g dietary fiber
	8.54 g protein	6.892 g fat	32.77 mg sodium	

LENTIL-TOMATO MINT SOUP

1½ cups lentils, rinsed

8 cups water

Two bay leaves

½ teaspoon thyme

¼ teaspoon sage

One red onion, diced

Three celery stalks, diced

Three garlic cloves, minced

2 tablespoons vegetable oil

Four fresh tomatoes, peeled and chunked, or one can whole tomatoes, chunked, with juice

3 tablespoons fresh mint

Salt and white pepper, to taste

Cook the lentils in the water with the spices until the lentils soften, for about 30 minutes. Do not drain.

Meanwhile, saute the onion, celery, and garlic in the cooking oil for about 5 minutes. Add the tomatoes to the onion and celery.

Add the vegetables and mint to the lentils and serve piping hot. Season if desired with white pepper and salt. Remove bay leaves before serving.

Serves 10

If you can hear the soup bubbling, the soup is probably cooking too hard and the temperature should be adjusted lower.

Nutritional analysis per serving	105 calories	15.69 g carbohydrate	0 mg cholesterol	4.007 g dietary fiber
	5.59 g protein	2.909 g fat	23.47 mg sodium	

MICROWAVE SPLIT PEA SOUP

1 pound split peas, rinsed

6 cups water

Three medium carrots, coarsely grated

One medium onion, chopped

1½ cups cooked ham, cut in bite-sized pieces

¼ teaspoon pepper

In a 3-quart or larger casserole, combine all the ingredients; cover and microwave on high (100-percent power) for 10 minutes. Reduce the power to medium (50-percent power) and microwave for 45 to 60 minutes, or until the vegetables are tender and the soup thickens. Stir two to three times during cooking.

Serves 8

Nutritional analysis per serving   157 calories   27.07 g carbohydrate   3.75 mg cholesterol   1.209 g dietary fiber
10.03 g protein   1.733 g fat   479.2 mg sodium

Middle European
Mushroom Pea Soup

2 quarts water

2 cups green split peas, rinsed

Two ham hocks or one baked ham bone

1 cup chopped onion

1 cup chopped carrots

1 cup chopped celery

One bay leaf

Two parsley sprigs

1½ teaspoons salt, if desired

¼ teaspoon ground black pepper

1 pound fresh mushrooms, rinsed, dried, and sliced, or two 6- to 8-ounce cans sliced mushrooms, drained

2 tablespoons butter or margarine

In a large saucepan or Dutch oven, combine the water, peas, ham hocks, onion, carrots, celery, bay leaf, parsley, salt, pepper, and half of the mushrooms. Bring to a boil. Simmer until the split peas are tender, usually for about 45 minutes, stirring occasionally. Remove the ham hocks, cut away the ham from the bones, and return the ham to the soup.

In a medium-sized skillet, melt the butter; add the remaining mushrooms and saute for 3 minutes. Stir the mushrooms into the soup. Serve the soup with black bread or croutons.

Serves 10

Nutritional analysis per serving   152 calories   20 g carbohydrate   8.3 mg cholesterol   0.97 g dietary fiber
     10.7 g protein   4.1 g fat   245.4 mg sodium

MULLIGATAWNY SOUP

2 cups yellow split peas, rinsed

2½ quarts cold or defatted chicken stock

One large carrot, grated

Two large potatoes, grated

One large onion, grated

½ to 1 teaspoon curry powder, as preferred

½ teaspoon salt

¼ teaspoon pepper

Breast of one chicken, chunked, optional

1 cup cooked brown rice

In a heavy kettle, add all the ingredients except for the cooked brown rice. Bring to a boil and simmer until the split peas are soft, usually for 45 minutes. The ingredients may be mashed, blended in a blender, or pressed through a strainer, however you prefer. Add the cooked rice, heat, and serve hot.

Serves 8

"Mulligatawny" is the name given to a soup made with chicken stock and flavored with curry. Its origins are with the British colonists in India.

Nutritional analysis per serving	232 calories	36.45 g carbohydrate	20.75 mg cholesterol	1.463 g dietary fiber
	16.84 g protein	2.687 g fat	160 mg sodium	

NEW YEAR'S EVE LENTIL SOUP

3 ounces diced bacon

¾ cup diced onion

¾ cup diced celery

¾ cup diced carrots

¾ cup flour

3½ quarts water

1 cup lentils, rinsed

2 teaspoons salt

Two bay leaves

1 teaspoon white thyme

4 tablespoons beef base

Pinch nutmeg

Pinch white pepper

¾ cup potatoes, diced

In a large skillet or saucepan, saute the bacon until soft. Add the onion, celery, and carrots; saute until the onion and celery are transparent.

Stirring constantly, add the flour to the saucepan. When the flour is blended smoothly with the bacon and vegetables, slowly add the water, stirring constantly. Then, add all the rest of the ingredients. Simmer for approximately 3 hours.

Serves 6

Many Greeks and Italians have long believed that eating lentils on the eve of the new year assures prosperity and good fortune.

Nutritional analysis per serving	252 calories	34.4 g carbohydrate	12.1 mg cholesterol	4.97 g dietary fiber
	12.7 g protein	7.4 g fat	831 mg sodium	

NUTMEG CREAM OF LENTIL SOUP

1 cup lentils, rinsed

1 quart chicken or ham stock

1 cup chopped onions

½ teaspoon thyme

1 tablespoon butter

1 tablespoon flour

2 cups whole milk

Salt and white pepper to taste

2 tablespoons lemon juice

½ cup cream

Nutmeg, grated

Combine the lentils, onion, thyme, and stock. Bring to a boil. Reduce the heat, cover, and simmer for 45 minutes.

In small batches, puree the well-cooked lentils with the stock in a blender, along with the onion and thyme.

Make a white sauce with the butter, flour, and milk. Add the seasonings. Combine the sauce with the puree and lemon juice. Heat *but do not boil.* Serve, topped with a spoonful of cream and grated nutmeg.

Serves 8

Nutritional analysis per serving · 145 calories · 16.14 g carbohydrate · 14.06 mg cholesterol · 2.819 g dietary fiber
8.079 g protein · 5.712 g fat · 263 mg sodium

ONION-LENTIL SOUP

4 cups sweet onion, peeled and
thinly sliced

Two garlic cloves, minced

¼ cup vegetable oil

1 cup lentils, rinsed

2 cups carrots, coarsely grated

1 teaspoon dried thyme, crumbled

One bay leaf

3 cups beef stock or broth

1 cup dry red wine

Salt and pepper to taste

Cheese Bread-Crumb Topping

In a large kettle, saute the onion and garlic in oil until the onion is golden but not browned. Add the lentils, carrots, herbs, and beef broth. Simmer, covered for 45 minutes, stirring occasionally. Add the wine and simmer for 5 minutes longer. Adjust the seasonings. Remove the bay leaf. Serve with Cheese Bread-Crumb Topping.

Serves 6

CHEESE BREAD-CRUMB TOPPING

1 cup soft bread crumbs

3 tablespoons vegetable margarine

½ cup cheddar cheese, grated

Saute bread crumbs in vegetable margarine until the crumbs are golden. Place in a small bowl and mix in cheddar cheese.

Nutritional analysis per serving   240 calories   25.73 g carbohydrate   0.303 mg cholesterol   6.2 g dietary fiber
    8.548 g protein   9.718 g fat   452.2 mg sodium

OVEN-BAKED SPLIT PEA SOUP

1 pound yellow or green split peas, rinsed

8 cups water

1½ cups sliced carrots

1½ cups sliced celery

One onion, minced

2 teaspoons dried thyme, crushed

1 teaspoon celery seed

¼ teaspoon pepper

One bay leaf

1 pound fully cooked kielbasa (Polish smoked sausage), sliced ¼-inch-thick

Salt to taste

In a 4½-quart Dutch oven, combine the split peas, water, carrots, celery, onion, thyme, celery seed, pepper, and bay leaf. Bake covered in a 350-degree oven for 2 hours.

Add the sausage and bake 30 minutes more, until the sausage is heated through. Remove the bay leaf.

Serve hot.

Serves 8

Nutritional analysis per serving	309 calories	25.94 g carbohydrate	37.07 mg cholesterol	1.083 g dietary fiber
	16.16 g protein	16.1 g fat	621.8 mg sodium	

PUREE OF PEA SOUP BOMBAY

2 tablespoons margarine

Four green onions, chopped

2 cups fresh, chopped spinach

One lettuce head, chopped

1 to 2 tablespoons chopped, fresh mint

2 cups green split peas, rinsed

4 cups water

2 cups milk

Salt and pepper to taste

1 cup carrots, diced thin, boiled in water until done, and drained (or leave raw and dice small)

Heat the margarine, add the onion, spinach, lettuce, and mint, and cook for a few minutes. Add the split peas and water, and cook on medium heat until the peas are tender. When cooked, blend in a food processor or blender.

Add the milk, salt, and pepper to the soup. Garnish with hot, boiled carrots and a thin ribbon of cream. Serve hot.

Serves 6 to 8

In recipes calling for potatoes, do not use a baking potato but rather any of the more firm varieties for the best results.

Nutritional analysis per serving	205 calories	31.17 g carbohydrate	9.429 mg cholesterol	1.749 g dietary fiber
	12.89 g protein	4.288 g fat	77.24 mg sodium	

SAMBAR SOUTH INDIAN VEGETABLE STEW

1 cup split peas, rinsed

3 cups water

One medium onion, chopped

One green pepper, chopped

Two carrots, sliced

Two potatoes, cut in 1-inch cubes

Half head cauliflower, or one
10-ounce package frozen cauliflower

2 tablespoons corn oil

¼ teaspoon mustard seed

½ teaspoon turmeric

1 tablespoon lemon juice

1 teaspoon salt

2 cups water

Combine the split peas and water in a large saucepan and cook, lightly covered, for 30 to 45 minutes, until tender. Meanwhile, prepare the vegetables and set aside.

Heat the oil in large frying pan. Add the mustard seed and cover with a lid until the seeds are almost finished popping. Add all the remaining ingredients (except the split peas) to the frying pan and cook until the vegetables are tender-crisp, for 10 to 15 minutes.

Add the vegetables to the cooked split peas and cook for another 15 minutes or until tender. Add more water to the stew if necessary. Serve the stew over rice. Warm pita bread and Indian chutney are nice accompaniments.

Serves 4

Nutritional analysis per serving 653.9 calories 131.7 g carbohydrate 0 mg cholesterol 8.911 g dietary fiber
18.74 g protein 8.282 g fat 589.7 mg sodium

SOUTHWESTERN LENTIL SOUP

1½ cups lentils, rinsed

6 cups water

½ teaspoon black pepper

½ teaspoon cumin

½ teaspoon mint, thyme, or oregano

Three bay leaves

¼ cup chopped, mild green chilies, pureed in a food processor or blender

One bell pepper, deveined, seeded, and cut into chunks

One carrot, diced

¼ cup fresh lime juice

2 tablespoons olive oil

Place the first seven ingredients into a large cooking pot; bring to a boil, cover, and simmer until the lentils are tender. Puree 1 cup of the cooked lentils with the green chilies in a blender and add to the soup. Add the finely chopped vegetables to the soup and cook until the vegetables are tender but not overcooked.

Just before serving, stir in the lime juice and olive oil. Serve piping hot.

Serves 4 to 6

Single or small households? You can still make up a pot of lentil or split pea soup. Enjoy some one day, then freeze the rest in single serving sizes for reheating in the microwave or in a saucepan. Add a little liquid for quicker saucepan reheating.

Nutritional analysis per serving | 191 calories | 27.69 g carbohydrate | 0 mg cholesterol | 6.629 g dietary fiber
| 10.1 g protein | 5.6 g fat | 90.4 mg sodium |

PALOUSE SOUP

1 cup green split peas, rinsed

1 cup lentils, rinsed

4 cups water

2 cups diced, cooked ham

One small onion, finely chopped

1 cup chopped carrot

1 cup chopped celery

Two garlic cloves, minced

Six parsley sprigs, chopped

4 tablespoons instant potatoes, optional

2 teaspoons salt

½ teaspoon pepper

½ teaspoon coriander

½ teaspoon ground cumin

¼ teaspoon turmeric

¼ teaspoon marjoram leaves

3 cups milk

Cook the peas and lentils in the water in a 5-quart kettle for about 20 minutes. Add all the other ingredients except for the milk, cover, and simmer for about 30 minutes, or until the vegetables are tender. Just before serving, add the milk and serve hot.

Serves 6 to 8

Nutritional analysis per serving

225 calories	32.45 g carbohydrate	18.43 mg cholesterol	4.091 g dietary fiber
14.3 g protein	5.188 g fat	763.6 mg sodium	

SPLIT PEA DILL SOUP

2 cups green split peas, rinsed

4 cups water

One large onion, chopped

Two carrots, chopped

Two celery stalks, sliced

3 tablespoons vegetable oil

⅔ cup fresh dill, snipped

4 cups beef or chicken stock

Pepper to taste

Soy sauce to taste

One meaty ham bone

Combine the peas with the water in a stock pot. Bring to a boil, reduce the heat, and simmer for 10 minutes.

Pour the oil into a skillet and cook the onion, carrots, and celery until the onion is golden. Add the vegetables to the peas in the stock pot, along with the dill, stock, pepper, soy sauce, and ham bone. Bring to a boil, reduce the heat, and simmer for 1 hour.

Remove the ham bone and take the meat off, chopping it up. Puree the soup in a blender; return it to the pot, and add the chopped ham.

Garnish the soup with a slice of lemon, sliced scallions, or a sprig of dill.

Serves 6

| Nutritional analysis per serving | 436 calories | 46.86 g carbohydrate | 37.2 mg cholesterol | 1.774 g dietary fiber |
| | 29.54 g protein | 17.37 g fat | 408.6 mg sodium | |

SPLIT PEA SOUP MILANO

1 cup split peas, rinsed

5 cups water

Five bouillon cubes or 5 teaspoons beef bouillon granules

Dash pepper

2 tablespoons olive oil

¼ pound Italian sausage

1 cup chopped celery

½ cup chopped onion

One garlic clove, minced

½ cup sweet red pepper, minced

¼ cup dry red wine or hot water

Grated Parmesan cheese

In a large saucepan or pot, combine the peas, water, bouillon, and pepper. Heat to boiling; reduce the heat, cover, and simmer until the peas are tender, stirring occasionally, for about 30 minutes.

Meanwhile, cook the sausage in the oil in a skillet over medium heat until it is no longer pink, breaking it into small pieces with the back of a spoon. Add the celery, onion, garlic, and red pepper, and saute until the onion is tender and translucent, for about 5 minutes.

Add the sausage-vegetable mixture to the peas along with the wine, and simmer for 10 to 15 minutes to blend the flavors.

Sprinkle with Parmesan cheese and serve.

Serves 5

White pepper is more immature when harvested than black pepper and also has a different flavor.

Nutritional analysis per serving   230 calories   19.43 g carbohydrate   17.84 mg cholesterol   0.708 g dietary fiber
12.50 g protein   11.94 g fat   527.4 mg sodium

SPLIT PEA SOUP WITH KIELBASA

1 cup green or yellow split peas or lentils, rinsed

4 cups water

One ham hock or meaty ham bone

One small bay leaf

⅓ cup chopped onion

⅓ cup chopped celery

⅓ cup chopped carrots

½ teaspoon salt

One small garlic clove, if desired

One kielbasa sausage (about ¾ pound)

Combine all the ingredients except for the sausage in a kettle with a tight lid. Bring to a boil. Reduce the heat and simmer, covered, for 2 hours, stirring occasionally. Remove the ham hock or bone and cool slightly. Cut the ham off of the bone, dice the meat, add it to the soup, and heat thoroughly.

Wash the kielbasa. Slash at 1-inch intervals about a fourth of the way through. Add to the soup.

Remove the bay leaf from the soup before serving. To serve the kielbasa, remove it from the soup and cut it into slices. Add the slices to each serving of soup.

Note: Split pea soups are very thick and may need thinning. To thin split pea soup, heat it slowly and stir in a small amount of stock, water, light cream, or undiluted evaporated milk.

Serves 4 or 5

Nutritional analysis per serving	327 calories	21.03 g carbohydrate	47.49 mg cholesterol	0.742 g dietary fiber
	16.49 g protein	19.82 g fat	1007 mg sodium	

SPLIT PEA STEW

2 cups water

1 cup yellow split peas, rinsed

One medium onion, chopped

½ pound sliced, fresh mushrooms, or one 4-ounce can mushroom pieces

1 teaspoon dried basil

One bay leaf

One chicken bouillon cube or ½ teaspoon salt

Two celery stalks, chopped

Two carrots, sliced

One can (1 pound) stewed tomatoes

4 tablespoons vegetable oil

2 tablespoons vinegar

Bring the water to a boil. Add the split peas and boil gently for 5 minutes. Remove the peas from the heat and let stand for 30 minutes. Do not drain.

Saute the onion, mushrooms, and basil in the oil, until the onion is limp but not browned. Add the split peas and remaining ingredients, except for the vinegar, and simmer gently for about 30 minutes. Remove the bay leaf and add the vinegar, just before serving.

Serves 8

Nutritional analysis per serving	156 calories	19.5 g carbohydrate	0 mg cholesterol	1.8 g dietary fiber
	5.5 g protein	7.3 g fat	313 mg sodium	

SUPERBOWL SUNDAY STEW

1 pound stew beef

Three slices bacon

One medium onion, cut in eighths

6 cups water

1 cup green split peas, rinsed

Juice of one lime

1 teaspoon salt

¼ teaspoon nutmeg

¼ teaspoon turmeric

One can (16 ounces) whole kernel corn, drained

One can (16 ounces) julienned carrots, drained

In a Dutch oven, brown the stew beef with the bacon. Drain off the excess fat. Add the onion and 2 cups of the water, and simmer for 1 hour. Add the rest of the water, split peas, lime juice, salt, nutmeg, and turmeric, and simmer for 1 hour more. Add the corn and carrots, and reheat.

Serves 8

Pulse is another name for a legume, the edible seed of a legume plant.

Nutritional analysis per serving	267 calories	21.79 g carbohydrate	56.03 mg cholesterol	1.36 g dietary fiber
	23.07 g protein	10.34 g fat	725.8 mg sodium	

SWEDISH LENTIL STEW WITH SALT COD

1 pound salt cod or fresh whitefish*

Water

3 onions, finely chopped

Olive oil for sauteing

1 cup lentils, rinsed

2 tablespoons vinegar

1 cup red wine

1 bay leaf

Pinch thyme

Sugar to taste

Pepper to taste

1 cup (½ pound) potatoes, diced

* When salt cod is used, soak it in cold water for at least 12 hours, changing the water three or four times. Drain the cod and rinse it under cold water.

In a saucepan, add enough fresh water to cover the fish by 1 inch. Bring to a boil, reduce the heat, and simmer uncovered for about 20 minutes, or until the fish flakes when prodded with a fork. Drain the fish, remove the skin and any bones, and separate into coarse flakes. Set the fish aside.

Saute the onions in the oil; combine with the lentils, vinegar, red wine, herbs, sugar and pepper, and cover with water. Put the potatoes on top and cook for 30 minutes to 1 hour until the lentils and potatoes are tender. Add the fish to the stew about 20 minutes before the end of the cooking period.

Garnish each serving with fresh or dried parsley or chives.

Serves 6

Nutritional analysis per serving   228 calories   25.57 g carbohydrate   41.58 mg cholesterol   4.564 g dietary fiber
         24.02 g protein   0.843 g fat   107.9 mg sodium

THICK LENTIL SOUP

Two slices bacon, diced

1 cup chopped onions

1 cup diced carrots

Half clove garlic, minced

7 cups cold water

4 cups beef broth

One can (6 ounces) tomato paste

1 to 2 cups diced, raw potatoes

1 pound dry lentils, rinsed

Two whole cloves

Two bay leaves

2 tablespoons red wine vinegar

1 pound sliced smoked turkey sausage, diced

1 teaspoon salt

In a large soup kettle, saute the bacon, onions, carrots, and garlic until the onion is tender. Add the water, broth, tomato paste, potatoes, lentils, cloves, and bay leaves. Simmer covered for 1½ hours. Add the vinegar, turkey, and salt to the soup and cook for another half hour. Remove the bay leaves and cloves before serving.

Serves 12

Nutritional analysis per serving   159 calories   17.60 g carbohydrate   14.33 mg cholesterol   3.115 g dietary fiber

8.872 g protein   6.318 g fat   634.6 mg sodium

VEGETARIAN SPLIT PEA SOUP

2 cups split peas, rinsed

2 quarts water

1 cup sliced celery

½ cup diced onion

1 cup chopped carrots

1 cup diced potato

One clove garlic, minced

One bay leaf

¼ cup snipped fresh parsley

½ teaspoon crushed oregano

½ teaspoon crushed basil

1 teaspoon dried Italian seasoning

½ teaspoon salt

Pinch cayenne

Combine all the ingredients in a Dutch oven. Bring to a boil. Reduce the heat, cover, and simmer for 1 hour or until the peas are cooked through. Remove the bay leaf from the soup before serving.

Serves 10

Roux is a term describing the combining of butter and flour into a smooth paste that may also be heated until browned before adding it to a soup for a thickening agent.

Nutritional analysis per serving   122.8 calories   23.90 g carbohydrate   0.000 mg cholesterol   0.997 g dietary fiber
7.166 g protein   0.517 g fat   126.4 mg sodium

WASHINGTON STATE REAL LENTIL SOUP

1 tablespoon safflower oil

One onion, coarsely chopped

Two celery stalks, chopped

One small bell pepper, chopped

One clove garlic, minced

Two small tomatoes, peeled and diced

1 teaspoon dry basil

1 teaspoon dry oregano

1 teaspoon paprika

½ teaspoon ground fennel

One large or two small bay leaves

1 cup lentils, rinsed

6 cups chicken flavor bouillon

12 ounces vegetable juice cocktail

1 cup diced carrots

½ cup diced turnip

1 cup diced potato

In a large pot, heat the oil and add the onion, celery, bell pepper, garlic, tomatoes, basil, oregano, paprika, fennel, and bay leaves. Let simmer for 10 minutes; then, add the lentils.

Add the bouillon and vegetable juice cocktail to the soup, and simmer for about 1 hour, adding water as needed. During the last 20 minutes, add the carrot, turnip, and potato to the soup and continue cooking.

Serves 9

Nutritional analysis per serving | 134 calories | 19.97 g carbohydrate | 0.667 mg cholesterol | 4.358 g dietary fiber
8.003 g protein | 2.714 g fat | 691.5 mg sodium

SALADS

ANY BEAN SALAD –
BUT MAKE IT WITH LENTILS!

1 cup lentils, rinsed

2 cups undrained, cut green, yellow, or kidney beans, or chickpeas

One medium onion, thinly sliced

½ cup sliced celery

2 tablespoons chopped green pepper, optional

¼ cup sugar

¼ teaspoon celery seed or salt

⅛ teaspoon salt

⅛ teaspoon pepper

1 teaspoon soy sauce

¼ cup vinegar

Cook the lentils in 2 cups of water for 20 minutes; *do not drain*.

Combine all the ingredients, cover, and refrigerate overnight. Just before serving, drain well. This is a delicious salad to serve with seafood.

Serves 4

Many recipes call for lentils or split peas to be cooked to the al dente stage. This means that they are tender and firm, but not soft. Test for al dente doneness by removing several seeds from the cooking water after 10 to 15 minutes and tasting them.

Nutritional analysis per serving   167.1 calories   36.07 g carbohydrate   0 mg cholesterol   5.817 g dietary fiber
8.763 g protein   0.168 g fat   184.8 mg sodium

ARABIC LENTIL SALAD

1 pound lentils, rinsed

6 cups water

One large yellow onion, cut in thin slices

Half a large green bell pepper, seeded and cut into thin strips

Half a large red bell pepper, seeded and cut into thin strips

Two medium-sized tomatoes, coarsely chopped for garnish

MARINADE

¾ cup olive oil

3 tablespoons lemon juice

⅛ cup cider vinegar

One medium-sized garlic clove, minced

⅛ teaspoon black pepper

2½ teaspoons salt

¾ teaspoon cayenne pepper

1 teaspoon ground cumin

½ teaspoon dried thyme

⅛ teaspoon dry mustard

One can (6 ounces) sliced black olives

Gently boil the lentils in the water for 12 to 15 minutes, to al dente doneness. Rinse in cold water and drain well.

Combine all the marinade ingredients and add to the lentils. Let the salad marinate in the refrigerator for 1 hour, stirring occasionally.

Stir in the onion and green pepper strips to the marinated lentils. Serve the salad in a large bowl. Garnish with chopped tomato and serve with warm pita bread cut into wedges.

Serves 8

Nutritional analysis per serving   364.5 calories   29.66 g carbohydrate   0 mg cholesterol   7.666 g dietary fiber
11.42 g protein   25.24 g fat   844 mg sodium

BROCCOLI LENTIL SALAD

1 cup lentils, rinsed

2 cups water

Salt and pepper to taste

½ cup reduced-calorie ranch dressing

1 cup chopped celery

½ cup chopped green onions

1 cup chopped jicama (a tropical plant with edible roots), optional

2 cups chopped broccoli, blanched

Cook the lentils in the water for 20 to 25 minutes. Drain and season while still hot with the salt, pepper, and dressing. Refrigerate until chilled; then add the celery, onions, jicama, and broccoli.

Serves 6

Nutritional analysis per serving	152.8 calories	15.94 g carbohydrate	0 mg cholesterol	4.438 g dietary fiber
	6.95 g protein	7.73 g fat	158.6 mg sodium	

CHICKEN LENTIL SALAD

½ cup lentils, rinsed

1 cup water

2 tablespoons oil

4 cups diced, cooked chicken

2 cups diced apples

1½ cups diced celery

1 cup diced pineapple

Cook the lentils in the water for 20 minutes; drain. Heat the oil in a skillet; add the lentils and saute until lightly browned. Cool. Combine with the remaining ingredients. Toss with mayonnaise and a touch of lemon juice.

Serves 5

Nutritional analysis per serving	291 calories	20.97 g carbohydrate	0 mg cholesterol	2.943 g dietary fiber
	13.88 g protein	17.33 g fat	571.3 mg sodium	

Colorful Peas and Sausage Salad

¾ cup split peas, rinsed

2 cups water

⅓ cup olive oil

2 tablespoons vinegar

¼ cup chopped parsley

1 tablespoon German hot mustard

Sugar, to taste

Salt and pepper, to taste

½ pound cooked, mildly spicy sausage, sliced

Two onions, finely chopped

Two tomatoes, chopped

Cook the peas in the water for 15 to 20 minutes, or until tender but retaining their shape. Drain and cool to room temperature.

Meanwhile, make a vinaigrette by whipping the olive oil, vinegar, parsley, mustard, sugar, salt, and pepper, until combined. Pour over the peas, sausage, onions, and tomatoes to marinate. Toss lightly and chill.

This salad is also very good warm.

Serves 6

Nutritional analysis per serving   331.2 calories   17.21 g carbohydrate   31.98 mg cholesterol   1.531 g dietary fiber

12.62 g protein   24.31 g fat   530.3 mg sodium

CRANBERRY SALAD

½ cup lentils, rinsed

1 cup water

One package strawberry-flavored gelatin

1½ cups boiling water

1 cup cranberry sauce

One small can (8 ounces) crushed pineapple

½ cup chopped celery

Cook the lentils in the 1 cup of water for 30 minutes; drain.

Mix the gelatin in the boiling water. Add the lentils, cranberry sauce, pineapple, and celery. Let set. Top this salad with whipped topping and grated cheese, if desired.

Serves 4

Nutritional analysis per serving	255.3 calories	61.15 g carbohydrate	0 mg cholesterol	4.452 g dietary fiber
	6.421 g protein	0.18 g fat	37.01 mg sodium	

LENTIL AND WALNUT SALAD

2 cups lentils, rinsed

4 cups water

¼ cup red wine vinegar

¾ cup extra-virgin olive oil

½ tablespoon dry mustard

½ teaspoon salt

¼ teaspoon white pepper

Two bunches scallions, thinly sliced

2 cups coarsely chopped walnuts

Cook the lentils in the water for 20 to 25 minutes, or until barely tender. Drain.

Whisk together the vinegar, oil, mustard, salt, and pepper to form a vinaigrette. While the lentils are still warm, combine with the scallions and walnuts in a large bowl and pour the dressing over all. Toss and chill until serving time.

Serves 10

Nutritional analysis per serving	326.5 calories	18.37 g carbohydrate	0 mg cholesterol	4.901 g dietary fiber
	10.44 g protein	25.28 g fat	131.2 mg sodium	

CRUNCHY PEA SALAD

1½ cups split peas, rinsed

3 cups water

1½ cups instant rice

One can water chestnuts, diced

Three bunches green onions

½ cup chopped celery

1 cup "cholesterol-free" mayonnaise

½ cup chili sauce

A few drops Tabasco sauce

1 tablespoon horseradish, optional

¼ cup red sweet pepper sauce, optional

Cook the split peas in the water for 25 to 30 minutes. Watch closely, because they need to be quite tender but not mushy. Drain, rinse, and chill. Prepare the instant rice, drain, and chill.

Combine the peas and rice with the water chestnuts, green onions, and celery. Make a dressing by combining the mayonnaise, chili sauce, Tabasco sauce, horseradish, and pepper sauce. This salad needs to be zesty.

Serves 12

Soluble fiber, which is abundant in split peas and lentils, has been found to help in decreasing serum glucose and cholesterol and decreasing insulin requirements for persons with diabetes.

Nutritional analysis per serving | 255.9 calories | 37.59 g carbohydrate | 0 mg cholesterol | 0.694 g dietary fiber
6.374 g protein | 9.338 g fat | 206.2 mg sodium

CURRIED LENTIL RICE SALAD

1 cup lentils, rinsed

2 cups water

1 cup plain yogurt

2 tablespoons lemon juice

2 tablespoons chopped fresh mint

1 tablespoon curry powder

Two cloves garlic, minced

Dash of freshly ground pepper

1 cup cooked rice

One medium cucumber, peeled, seeded, and sliced thin

1 cup chopped sweet red or green pepper

1 cup chopped green onion

Salt and pepper, to taste

Cook the lentils in the water for 20 minutes or until just barely tender. Drain, if necessary.

Combine the yogurt, lemon juice, mint, and seasonings. Add to the lentils along with all the remaining ingredients. Cover and chill several hours to blend the flavors.

Serves 6

Nutritional analysis per serving   223 calories   41.89 g carbohydrate   3.5 mg cholesterol   7.301 g dietary fiber
13.07 g protein   1.298 g fat   75.06 mg sodium

DEVILED HOT POTATO LENTIL SALAD

1 cup lentils, rinsed

2 cups water

1 cup plain yogurt

2 tablespoons Dijon-style mustard

½ teaspoon salt

1 teaspoon sugar

4 cups diced cooked potatoes

¼ cup chopped green onion

½ cup chopped dill pickles

Combine the lentils and the water, and cook for 20 minutes; drain. Combine the yogurt, mustard, salt, and sugar.

When ready to serve, heat the lentils and potatoes together. Combine the dressing, onion, and dill pickles. Toss with the potato-lentil mixture and serve immediately.

Serves 8

When preparing lentils for use other than in soups, simmer them in water to the al dente stage. Pour off cooking water and cover al dente lentils with warmed, seasoned or flavored liquids like bases, stocks, fruit juices, or salad dressings. Cool. During the cooling process, lentils absorb the flavors and some moisture of this secondary liquid. Delicious!

Nutritional analysis per serving	255.7 calories	26.57 g carbohydrate	87.25 mg cholesterol	5.178 g dietary fiber
	9.09 g protein	10.94 g fat	967.7 mg sodium	

GARDEN LENTIL TOSS

1 cup lentils

2 cups water

One head cauliflower, broken into florets

One bunch broccoli, broken into pieces

Two cucumbers, sliced and quartered, with peel left on

One large carrot, grated

½ cup chopped onion (purple onion is colorful)

Six to eight fresh mushrooms, sliced

½ cup sliced olives

Bring the lentils in the water to a boil and simmer for 20 minutes; drain and cool.

Toss the remaining ingredients and serve with Hidden Valley Ranch dressing.

Serves 6 to 8

If you eat lentils and split peas with rice or with products containing cereal grains, such as pasta, you obtain a complete high-quality protein equivalent to beef — with a fraction of the fat and cholesterol. Experiment by substituting lentils or split peas for all or a portion of the meat in your favorite recipe.

Nutritional analysis per serving	190 calories	23.03 g carbohydrate	0 mg cholesterol	7.062 g dietary fiber
	9.012 g protein	8.45 g fat	189.3 mg sodium	

GARNISHED LENTIL SALAD

1 pound (2⅓ cups) lentils, rinsed

5 cups water

½ cup smoked ham, diced

⅓ cup ripe olives, diced

¼ cup sweet red pepper, diced

¼ cup red onion, diced

Two cloves garlic, finely minced

¼ cup chopped Italian parsley

1 tablespoon oil

2 teaspoons lemon juice, freshly
squeezed

1 tablespoon peppercorns, coarsely
ground

2 teaspoons salt

Lettuce leaves, trimmed and
chilled, as needed

Four eggs, hard-cooked and finely
chopped

2 cups grapes in small clusters

12 parsley sprigs

Cook the lentils for 20 to 30 minutes or just until tender. Drain and cool to room temperature. Add the diced ham, vegetables, garlic, and parsley.

Combine the oil, lemon juice, and peppercorn; pour over the lentil salad and gently toss until mixed. Season to taste with salt. Serve at room temperature.

Individual serving: Arrange lettuce leaves on a serving plate and center with ½ cup lentil salad. Top with a sprinkling of chopped egg. Garnish with a grape cluster and parsley sprig.

Serves 12

Nutritional analysis per serving   166.8 calories   20.39 g carbohydrate   96.94 mg cholesterol   4.795 g dietary fiber
                                     11.35 g protein   5.518 g fat   591.8 mg sodium

LAGUNA BEACH LENTIL SALAD

½ cup lentils, rinsed

1 cup water

¼ teaspoon salt

Three sprigs parsley

Four sprigs basil

Two cloves garlic

¼ cup diced carrot

¼ cup diced red onion

1 tablespoon diced celery

⅓ cup virgin olive oil

2 ounces goat cheese

2 tablespoons snipped chives

2 tablespoons strong red wine vinegar

Freshly ground black pepper

Salt

One ripe tomato

Four to five basil leaves

Combine the lentils, water, and salt in a saucepan. Make a bouquet garni by tying two sprigs of parsley, two sprigs of basil, and one clove of garlic, unpeeled and slightly crushed, in a cheesecloth. Add the bouquet garni to the lentils and cook for 10 minutes.

Add the vegetables to the lentils and simmer for 10 to 15 minutes until the lentils are tender but retain their shape. If necessary, add hot water, ¼ cup at a time, to keep the lentils from sticking. There should be very little liquid when the lentils are done.

When done, discard the bouquet garni, toss the lentils with 2 tablespoons of the olive oil, and spread on baking sheets to cool. If the goat cheese tastes very strong, trim the outer rind to the chalk-white center. Crumble the cheese coarsely into a large bowl. Finely mince the remaining parsley, basil, and garlic cloves.

Combine the lentil mixture with the cheese and minced parsley, basil, and garlic. Add the remainder of the olive oil, the red wine vinegar, and freshly ground black pepper. Toss well, taste for balance, and salt. Cover and refrigerate for at least 2 hours.

Remove the salad from the refrigerator about 1 hour before serving and taste again for balance in the vinaigrette; you may need more vinegar, oil, salt, or pepper. Just before serving, garnish with tomatoes cut in wedges, and basil leaves cut in very fine strips.

Serves 6

Nutritional analysis per serving	185.3 calories	8.366 g carbohydrate	8.438 mg cholesterol	1.964 g dietary fiber
	4.267 g protein	15.58 g fat	207.7 mg sodium	

HERBED LENTIL AND RICE SALAD

1 cup lentils, rinsed

2 cups water

1 tablespoon crab boil seasoning mix (usually at the fish counter in your grocer's meat department)

1 cup cooked brown rice

1 cup chopped green pepper

½ cup chopped green onion

½ cup chopped fresh parsley

1 teaspoon grated lemon peel

⅓ cup lemon juice

¼ cup olive or salad oil

1 tablespoon chopped fresh marjoram or 2 teaspoons dried marjoram leaves, crumbled

Salt and pepper to taste

Cook the lentils in the water with the crab boil seasoning mix for 20 minutes or just until the lentils are barely tender. Drain, if necessary, and combine with the remaining ingredients. Cover the salad and chill for several hours or overnight to blend the flavors.

Serves 4

Both split peas and lentils have a mild flavor that readily absorbs and harmonizes with spices and herbs and provides an excellent complement to fish, fowl, and red meats.

Nutritional analysis per serving	296.2 calories	35.72 g carbohydrate	0 mg cholesterol	6.587 g dietary fiber
	9.771 g protein	13.93 g fat	300.7 mg sodium	

JAPANESE SPROUT SALAD

1 cup lentil sprouts*

Four carrots, grated

Four "burpless" cucumbers, unpeeled and cut in matchstick pieces (if using regular cucumbers, peel and seed first)

DRESSING

2 tablespoons white sesame seeds

4 tablespoons salad oil

½ cup sugar

1 cup rice vinegar

1 teaspoon salt

Make the dressing by heating the sesame seeds in the salad oil, just until the seeds are light brown. Remove from the heat and cool. Add the other dressing ingredients and blend thoroughly; refrigerate until needed.

Mix the sprouts, carrots, and cucumbers lightly. Pour the dressing over them, toss, and serve immediately or refrigerate for 1 to 2 hours.

Serves 6

* For how to make your own lentil sprouts, please see page *xi*.

What to do with those extra lentil sprouts? Saute them in a little olive oil, salt, and pepper to taste, and serve as a simple side dish.

Nutritional analysis per serving	216.5 calories	32.47 g carbohydrate	0 mg cholesterol	4.567 g dietary fiber
	3.44 g protein	10.99 g fat	378.8 mg sodium	

KALEIDOSCOPE SALAD

½ cup lentils, rinsed

1 cup water

½ cup diced celery

½ cup diced onion

One small purple cabbage, finely chopped

½ cup diced green pepper

One large carrot, grated

⅓ cup salad oil

⅔ cup white vinegar

½ cup sugar

Combine the lentils and water. Cook for 20 minutes and drain. Cool the lentils, combine with the remaining ingredients, and chill for several hours before serving.

Serves 4

Nutritional analysis per serving
221.2 calories
3.682 g protein
28.7 g carbohydrate
12.19 g fat
0 mg cholesterol
20.31 mg sodium
3.557 g dietary fiber

LENTIL AND BULGUR SALAD

1 cup lentils, rinsed

4 cups homemade broth or 4 cups water with one bouillon cube

1 cup bulgur

2 cups boiling water

½ cup finely chopped sweet Spanish or red onion

1 cup minced fresh parsley

½ cup thinly sliced scallions

DRESSING

Two cloves garlic, minced

1 tablespoon Dijon-style mustard

¼ cup chicken broth

1 tablespoon olive oil

2 tablespoons Aceto Balsamico vinegar or red wine vinegar

½ teaspoon Tabasco, or to taste

½ teaspoon Worcestershire sauce

1 teaspoon oregano

½ teaspoon dried basil

¼ teaspoon ground cumin

Salt to taste

Freshly ground black pepper to taste

Cook the lentils in the broth for 20 minutes. Let stand for 10 minutes longer and then drain. Meanwhile, put the bulgur in a heat-proof bowl and pour the boiling water over it; let the bulgur stand for 10 minutes and then drain.

Combine the lentils and bulgur in a large bowl. Add the onion and parsley. In a jar or small bowl, combine all the dressing ingredients and pour over the lentil mixture. Toss. Add the scallions at serving time and toss again.

Makes 6 cups

Nutritional analysis per serving | 211.3 calories | 39.35 g carbohydrate | 0.066 mg cholesterol | 9.369 g dietary fiber
8.919 g protein | 3.04 g fat | 241.6 mg sodium

Lentil Gelatin Salad

1 cup lentils, rinsed

2 cups water

3 ½ cups tomato juice

Two packages lemon-flavored gelatin

½ teaspoon seasoning salt

1 tablespoon vinegar

One can (8 ounces) shrimp

¼ cup chopped onion

¼ cup chopped celery

¼ cup chopped green pepper

Cook the lentils in the water for 20 to 25 minutes or until tender. Drain.

Heat half of the tomato juice and dissolve the gelatin in it. Stir in the seasoning salt, remaining tomato juice, and vinegar. Add the remaining ingredients and chill until set.

Serves 6

Research has shown there are two types of fiber — insoluble, or roughage, which promotes efficient working of the intestines, and soluble, which is the water soluble or gummy fiber abundantly present in legumes, oats, barley, and some fresh fruits. Legumes like lentils and split peas contribute more fiber than any other group of foods.

Nutritional analysis per serving

| 167.3 calories | 35.81 g carbohydrate | 18.5 mg cholesterol | 3.482 g dietary fiber |
| 8.978 g protein | 0.313 g fat | 720.6 mg sodium | |

LENTIL RICE SALAD WITH MUSTARD DRESSING

½ cup lentils, rinsed

1½ cups water

One tomato, chopped

¼ cup sliced green onion

½ cup diced celery

½ cup diced carrots

½ cup diced green pepper

1½ cups broccoli florets

1 tablespoon snipped fresh parsley

1½ cups cooked rice

MUSTARD DRESSING

¼ cup seasoned rice vinegar

1 tablespoon lemon juice

1½ teaspoons Dijon-style mustard

2½ tablespoons olive oil

Cook the lentils in the water for 20 minutes; drain and cool. Combine with the remaining salad ingredients. Mix together the ingredients for the mustard dressing. Toss the dressing with the salad. Chill for several hours or overnight.

Serves 7

Nutritional analysis per serving	137.1 calories	20.23 g carbohydrate	0 mg cholesterol	3.13 g dietary fiber
	4.162 g protein	5.046 g fat	34.75 mg sodium	

LENTIL SALAD PROVENCE

1 cup lentils, rinsed

2 cups water

Three to four cloves garlic, minced

½ cup minced onion

1 cup chopped, seeded tomatoes

1 cup chopped, seeded cucumber

¼ cup chopped fresh parsley

2 tablespoons olive oil

2 tablespoons chopped fresh oregano, or 1 teaspoon dried oregano leaves

4 ounces feta cheese, crumbled

Cook the lentils, garlic, and onion in the water for 20 minutes or just until the lentils are barely tender. Drain if necessary.

Toss the lentils with the remaining ingredients. Cover and chill for several hours to blend the flavors. Serve on lettuce leaves or in pita bread.

Serves 4

Nutritional analysis per serving   255.5 calories   24.03 g carbohydrate   25.31 mg cholesterol   5.736 g dietary fiber
    12.77 g protein   13.02 g fat   355.4 mg sodium

LENTIL SALAD WITH MINT DRESSING

1 cup lentils, rinsed

2 cups water

½ cup diced jicama

½ cup diced carrot

¼ cup diced red pepper

½ cup minced scallions

Salt and pepper

DRESSING

2 tablespoons chopped fresh mint

3 tablespoons red wine vinegar

¼ cup light whipping cream

½ cup olive oil

Cook the lentils in the water for 25 minutes. Drain. Mix the lentils while still warm with the vegetables. Add the salt and pepper to taste.

To prepare the dressing, combine the mint and vinegar. Whisk in the cream, and then the olive oil. Toss the dressing with the lentils and vegetables.

Serves 8

| Nutritional analysis per serving | 201.2 calories | 12.08 g carbohydrate | 8.281 mg cholesterol | 3.017 g dietary fiber |
| | 4.387 g protein | 15.85 g fat | 22.58 mg sodium | |

79

LENTIL SALAD WITH THYME DRESSING

1 cup lentils, rinsed

1¾ cups water

½ cup lemon juice

½ cup olive oil

One clove garlic

2 tablespoons chopped thyme

½ cup diced red pepper

½ cup diced green pepper

½ cup sliced zucchini

½ cup crumbled blue cheese

Salt and pepper to taste

Combine the lentils with the water and simmer for 20 minutes. Remove from the heat and let cool.

Whisk together the lemon juice, olive oil, garlic, and thyme. Toss with the lentil mixture. Add the red and green peppers, and zucchini. Cover and chill for 2 to 4 hours to blend the flavors. Just before serving, toss in the blue cheese.

Serves 6

Buzzing split peas for a minute in a food processor chops them a little to expose more surfaces and help shorten the cooking time.

Nutritional analysis per serving	274.4 calories	16.41 g carbohydrate	7.088 mg cholesterol	3.691 g dietary fiber
	7.764 g protein	20.86 g fat	154.9 mg sodium	

LENTIL SAUSAGE SALAD

1 pound sausage links

1½ cups lentils, rinsed

3 cups water

One large green bell pepper, seeded and diced

One sweet red onion, thinly sliced

Two large tomatoes, chopped

Garlic and Mustard Vinaigrette

Romaine lettuce leaves, for serving

Spinach leaves, for serving

Three hard-cooked eggs, quartered

Put the sausage in a skillet with enough water to cover. Cook over medium heat until thoroughly cooked. Meanwhile, combine the lentils with the 3 cups of water and cook for 20 minutes; drain and cool.

Put the lentils, green pepper, onion, and tomatoes into a medium-sized bowl. Add ¼ cup of the vinaigrette dressing and toss to coat.

Cut the sausage into thin slices and add to the salad. Add the remaining ¼ cup of the dressing. Mound the salad onto a bed of crisp romaine and spinach leaves, and garnish with the quartered eggs. Serve at room temperature.

GARLIC AND MUSTARD VINAIGRETTE

5 tablespoons olive oil

3 tablespoons red wine vinegar

½ teaspoon very finely chopped garlic

1 teaspoon Dijon-style mustard

½ teaspoon salt

¼ teaspoon pepper

Combine the ingredients in a glass jar with a tight-fitting lid and shake thoroughly to combine.

Serves 10

Nutritional analysis per serving   327.4 calories   15.44 g carbohydrate   119.2 mg cholesterol   3.655 g dietary fiber
16.07 g protein   22.72 g fat   741.2 mg sodium

MAINE LOBSTER LENTIL SALAD

One medium onion, diced

2 tablespoons sweet butter

2 cups Red Chief lentils

1½ teaspoons chopped fresh thyme

1 cup chicken stock, heated

1 cup hot water

Three (each 1¼ pounds) Maine lobsters

½ cup whipping cream

1 ounce Serrugar caviar

1 tablespoon lemon juice

Salt and pepper to taste

Olive oil vinaigrette, as needed

1 pound mixed lettuce leaves

In an ovenware saucepan, saute the onion in the butter until transparent. Add the lentils and thyme; saute for 1 minute. Stir in the stock and water, cover, and place in 350-degree oven for 7 to 10 minutes. Stir twice while baking. Remove the pan from the oven; the lentils should be al dente. Set aside to cool.

Cook the lobsters in boiling water for 7 to 8 minutes. Remove the meat from the tails and claws.

Whip the cream just until it coats a spoon. Add the caviar and lemon juice. Season to taste.

Slice the lobster claws lengthwise and the tails into thin medallions. Season with salt and pepper; brush with the vinaigrette.

Place the lentils in a mixing bowl and moisten with a small amount of the vinaigrette. Toss the lettuce with the vinaigrette and season to taste. Divide the lettuce among 12 plates. Divide the lentils and place on top of the lettuce. On each plate, arrange three or four medallions of lobster on top of the lentils, and then half of a lobster claw over the medallions. Divide and ladle a small amount of the caviar cream sauce around each serving of the lentils and lobster. Serve immediately.

Serves 12

Nutritional analysis per serving   270.1 calories   16.33 g carbohydrate   125.8 mg cholesterol   3.49 g dietary fiber
35.4 g protein   6.723 g fat   660.5 mg sodium

Excellent

LENTIL CONFETTI SALAD

½ cup lentils, rinsed

1½ cups water

1 cup cooked rice

½ cup Italian dressing

One small tomato, diced

¼ cup chopped green pepper

¼ cup chopped onion

2 tablespoons chopped celery

2 tablespoons sliced, pimiento-stuffed green olives

Cook the lentils in the water for 20 minutes or until tender; drain.

Meanwhile, combine the remaining ingredients. Add the lentils, toss, and chill.

Serves 6

Nutritional analysis per serving   231.3 calories   22.15 g carbohydrate   0 mg cholesterol   2.498 g dietary fiber
3.436 g protein   14.78 g fat   324.4 mg sodium

MOZZARELLA RICE SALAD

¾ cup lentils, rinsed

1½ cups water

3 cups cooked rice, cooled

1 cup diced tomato

1 cup chopped broccoli

2 cups shredded mozzarella cheese

¼ cup thinly sliced green onions, including tops

½ cup plain yogurt

¼ cup reduced-calorie sour cream

1 tablespoon Dijon-style mustard

½ teaspoon sugar

½ teaspoon salt

⅛ teaspoon ground red pepper

Lettuce leaves

Cook the lentils in the water for 20 minutes or until just barely tender; drain and cool. Combine the lentils, rice, tomato, broccoli, cheese, and green onion in a large mixing bowl. Blend the remaining ingredients, except for the lettuce. Toss with the lentil and rice mixture, and chill. Serve on lettuce leaves.

Serves 6

Nutritional analysis per serving   299.7 calories   39.81 g carbohydrate   26.77 mg cholesterol   4.232 g dietary fiber

17.38 g protein   7.849 g fat   430.9 mg sodium

MEDITERRANEAN LENTIL SALAD

1½ cups lentils, rinsed

3 cups water

One each: red, green, and yellow bell peppers, cut in strips

10 cherry tomatoes

¼ cup toasted pine nuts, optional

½ cup black olives

8 ounces feta cheese, cubed

2 tablespoons fresh, chopped basil

¼ teaspoon dried oregano

DRESSING

⅔ cup olive oil

3 tablespoons red wine vinegar

2 tablespoons chopped fresh basil

2 tablespoons chopped green onion

1 teaspoon salt

¼ teaspoon black pepper

Two cloves garlic

Cook the lentils in the water for 20 minutes or until just tender. Rinse in cold water.

Blend the dressing ingredients in a blender. Toss the salad ingredients with the dressing. Adjust the seasoning, if desired. Chill.

Serves 10

Nutritional analysis per serving:	281.5 calories	15.9 g carbohydrate	20.25 mg cholesterol	3.9 g dietary fiber
	8.95 g protein	21.8 g fat	562 mg sodium	

PASTA SALAD PRIMAVERA

1 cup green split peas, rinsed

2 cups water

¼ cup white wine vinegar

One garlic clove, minced

1 tablespoon Dijon-style mustard

¼ teaspoon crushed red pepper flakes

½ teaspoon salt

¼ teaspoon pepper

¼ cup olive oil

4 cups cooked corkscrew or other small pasta

1½ cups diced red or green pepper

1½ cups thinly sliced green onion

In a saucepan, combine the peas with the water. Cover and simmer for 10 to 15 minutes, or until the peas are just tender but still hold their shape.

Meanwhile, combine the vinegar, garlic, mustard, red pepper, salt, and pepper. Beat in the oil. Add the remaining ingredients and peas. Toss and chill.

Serves 8

Puree cooked lentils and split peas to create pates, spreads, or dips, or add to quick breads, muffins, or carrot or zucchini cake for extra moistness and fiber.

Nutritional analysis per serving	220.8 calories	32.13 g carbohydrate	0 mg cholesterol	1.548 g dietary fiber
	7.96 g protein	7.706 g fat	162.3 mg sodium	

PEPPERONI SALAD

1 cup lentils, rinsed

2 cups water

1 cup long-grain brown rice

3 cups water

1 cup pepperoni, casing removed, sliced thin, and chopped

One small fennel bulb, chopped

Four scallions, green and white parts, sliced thin

Four large garlic cloves, boiled for 10 minutes, drained, and peeled

¼ cup red wine vinegar

1 tablespoon Dijon-style mustard

Salt and pepper to taste

⅓ cup corn, peanut, or safflower oil

Cook the lentils in the 2 cups of water for 30 minutes; drain. Cook the rice in the 3 cups of water for 25 minutes or until tender. Drain the rice in a colander and refresh under cold water. Set aside to drain and cool.

Combine the cooled rice with the lentils in a bowl along with the pepperoni, fennel, and scallions.

In a blender, puree the garlic with the vinegar, mustard, salt, and pepper. With the motor running, add the oil in a stream until the dressing is combined and emulsified. Pour the dressing over the salad and toss well. Taste for seasoning.

You can make this salad a day in advance and refrigerate. Remove from the refrigerator at least an hour before serving.

Serves 6

Nutritional analysis per serving   361.6 calories   33.79 g carbohydrate   0 mg cholesterol   4.622 g dietary fiber
11.45 g protein   20.94 g fat   439.9 mg sodium

PICNIC SALAD

1 cup lentils, rinsed

2 cups water

2 cups cooked or canned black-eyed peas

2 cups hot, cooked rice

½ cup chopped celery

½ cup chopped sweet pepper

½ cup chopped red onion

1 cup chopped bread-and-butter pickles

1 teaspoon salt

½ teaspoon pepper

⅓ cup mayonnaise

4 ounces cubed white or yellow cheese

Lettuce leaves

Combine the lentils with the water and cook for 30 minutes; drain. Combine the hot lentils, black-eyed peas, hot rice, celery, sweet pepper, onion, and pickles. Sprinkle with the salt and pepper, and stir. Then, fold in the mayonnaise and chill for 2 hours or longer. Serve in a lettuce-lined bowl and sprinkle cubed cheese on top.

Serves 8

Nutritional analysis per serving   288.6 calories   33.93 g carbohydrate   19 mg cholesterol   7.388 g dietary fiber

11.89 g protein   12.2 g fat   607.4 mg sodium

RAMEN SPROUT SALAD

4 cups chopped cabbage

2 tablespoons sesame seeds

½ cup sliced almonds

One package Ramen noodles, any flavor

Four green onions, thinly sliced

1 cup lentil sprouts*

DRESSING

2 tablespoons sugar

3 tablespoons vinegar

Seasoning packet from noodles

½ cup oil

1 teaspoon salt

Combine the salad ingredients and stir together. Combine the dressing ingredients. Toss the dressing with the salad 1 hour before serving.

Serves 10

* See page *xi* for how to sprout lentils.

Lentil sprouts are very high in Vitamins C and E and are delicious in salads.

Nutritional analysis per serving	229.5 calories	12.72 g carbohydrate	0 mg cholesterol	2.906 g dietary fiber
	3.928 g protein	19.7 g fat	375.8 mg sodium	

RICKSHAW SALAD

DRESSING

1 tablespoon margarine

2 tablespoons flour

1 tablespoon sugar

2 tablespoons vinegar

1 teaspoon soy sauce

½ teaspoon dry mustard

¼ teaspoon salt

¾ cup milk

SALAD

8 cups torn spinach leaves

8 ounces frozen, imitation crabmeat, thawed

2 cups sliced, fresh mushrooms

2 cups lentil sprouts*

Three green onions, sliced

½ cup sliced celery

Melt the margarine in the microwave or a saucepan. Stir in the remaining dressing ingredients. Microwave on high for 2 to 3 minutes to thicken, stirring once or twice, or continue to cook to thicken in the saucepan, stirring constantly. Refrigerate until cool.

Combine the salad ingredients in a large salad bowl. Just before serving, add the cooled dressing and toss to coat evenly.

Serves 6

* See page *xi* for how to sprout lentils.

Nutritional analysis per serving | 93.9 calories | 19.54 g carbohydrate | 11.69 mg cholesterol | 4.570 g dietary fiber
11.04 g protein | 9.684 g fat | 631.0 mg sodium

SALAD ITALIANO

1 cup lentils, rinsed

1 cup diced carrots

1 cup diced red onion

Two (or more!) large garlic cloves, minced

One bay leaf

½ teaspoon dried thyme

2 tablespoons olive oil

2 tablespoons lemon juice

½ cup diced celery

¼ cup chopped, fresh parsley

1 teaspoon salt, or to taste

¼ teaspoon freshly ground pepper

Combine the lentils, carrots, onion, garlic, bay leaf, and thyme in a saucepan. Add enough water to cover by at least 1 inch. Bring to a boil; reduce the heat and simmer, uncovered, until the lentils are tender but not mushy, 15 to 20 minutes. Drain and remove the bay leaf.

Add the oil, lemon juice, celery, parsley, salt, and pepper. Toss to mix and serve at room temperature.

Serves 4

Lentils harmonize particularly well with the flavors of the Mediterranean countries (where they are widely eaten): garlic, sweet basil, lemon, feta or Parmesan cheeses, olive oil, tarragon, salami, tomato . . .

Nutritional analysis per serving   197.9 calories   27.19 g carbohydrate   0 mg cholesterol   6.843 g dietary fiber
                                     9.112 g protein   6.984 g fat   576.7 mg sodium

SALAD SONORA

1 cup lentils, rinsed

2 cups water

One medium onion, chopped

Two garlic cloves, minced

1½ teaspoons chili powder

½ teaspoon ground cumin

1 cup fresh or frozen corn kernels

1 cup salsa

One can (4 ounces) chopped green chilies

½ cup chopped green pepper

½ cup sliced ripe olives

½ cup chopped fresh cilantro, or 2 teaspoons dry cilantro

Combine the lentils, water, onion, garlic, chili powder, and cumin. Cook for 20 minutes or until the lentils are just barely tender. Drain, if necessary.

Combine the lentil mixture with all the remaining ingredients, cover, and chill for several hours or overnight to blend the flavors. Serve in a taco "bowl," on thinly sliced fresh vegetables, or with tortilla chips.

Serves 12

Nutritional analysis per serving   156.1 calories   26.01 g carbohydrate   0 mg cholesterol   5.407 g dietary fiber
    8.079 g protein   5.436 g fat   300.4 mg sodium

SALAD VINAIGRETTE

⅔ cup lentils, rinsed

1½ cups water

Two large tomatoes, peeled, seeded, and chopped coarsely

½ cup scallions, sliced (both white and green parts)

⅓ cup chopped, fresh parsley

½ teaspoon oregano

3 tablespoons light Tuscan olive oil

2 teaspoons fresh lemon juice

2 teaspoons red wine vinegar

Salt and pepper to taste

Cook the lentils in the water for 20 minutes and drain. Cool.

In a large serving bowl, gently toss the lentils with the tomatoes, scallions, ¼ cup of the parsley, and oregano. Combine the olive oil, lemon juice, and wine vinegar, and drizzle over the salad. Season with salt and pepper to taste and toss. Serve at room temperature or chilled, garnished with the remaining parsley.

Serves 4

Nutritional analysis per serving — 175.4 calories — 6.1 g protein — 16.79 g carbohydrate — 10.3 g fat — 0 mg cholesterol — 27.36 mg sodium — 4.421 g dietary fiber

SUMMER LENTIL SALAD

1 quart water

2 cups lentils, rinsed

Two parsley sprigs

One bay leaf

One sliver lemon peel

2 tablespoons salad oil

1 tablespoon vinegar

1 tablespoon sugar

½ teaspoon salt

½ teaspoon pepper

One small onion, minced

Combine the water, lentils, parsley, bay leaf, and lemon peel. Cook for 20 minutes; drain. Discard the parsley, bay leaf, and lemon peel. Cool.

Combine the salad oil, vinegar, sugar, salt, pepper, and onion. Add to the lentils. Serve hot or cold, with sliced tomatoes and cold sliced beef.

Serves 6

No one knows just who discovered lentils and split peas, but archaeologists say they were among the first plants to be domesticated. Ancient Egyptians, Hebrews, Greeks, and Romans cultivated them. Today they are grown and eaten on every continent in the world.

Nutritional analysis per serving	192.6 calories	29.25 g carbohydrate	0 mg cholesterol	6.797 g dietary fiber
	10.84 g protein	4.582 g fat	218.1 mg sodium	

SWEET 'N SOUR FRUIT AND LENTIL SALAD

½ cup lentils, rinsed

1 cup water

1 cup cooked rice

One can pineapple tidbits, drained

One can mandarin oranges, drained and halved

1 cup chopped apple

⅔ cup chopped walnuts

DRESSING

1 cup Miracle Whip Salad Dressing

3 tablespoons pineapple juice

2 teaspoons honey

1 teaspoon sugar

⅛ teaspoon salt

Cook the lentils in the water for 20 minutes or until just barely tender; drain. Combine the lentils with the cooked rice. Mix the dressing ingredients together and add to the lentil-rice mixture while still hot. Toss and refrigerate immediately until cool. Add the pineapple, mandarin oranges, apple, and walnuts. Toss again and serve.

Serves 6

Nutritional analysis per serving	241.9 calories	34.95 g carbohydrate	21.33 mg cholesterol	3.817 g dietary fiber
	7.835 g protein	9.125 g fat	368.1 mg sodium	

TURKEY ROTINI SALAD

½ cup split peas, rinsed

1 cup water

4 cups cooked rotini pasta, cooled

3½ ounces diced, cooked turkey

¼ cup diced green pepper

½ cup grated carrot

2 tablespoons sliced black olive

2 tablespoons sliced green onion

2 tablespoons grated Parmesan cheese

¼ cup snipped, fresh parsley

DRESSING

8 ounces nonfat yogurt

Two garlic cloves, minced

1½ tablespoons olive oil

2 tablespoons tarragon white vinegar

¾ teaspoon dry mustard

½ teaspoon crushed oregano

½ teaspoon crushed basil

¼ teaspoon crushed red pepper

¼ teaspoon salt

Cook the peas in the water for 20 minutes; drain and cool. Combine the peas with the remaining salad ingredients.

Meanwhile, combine all the dressing ingredients together and toss with the salad. Chill for several hours before serving.

Serves 5

Nutritional analysis per serving
319.4 calories
18.73 g protein
45.93 g carbohydrate
7.619 g fat
17.94 mg cholesterol
228.4 mg sodium
2.325 g dietary fiber

WARM SALAD OF LENTILS, LAMB LOIN, AND CHEVRE

1¼ cups lentils, rinsed

One carrot, finely diced

One onion, pared and finely diced

2½ tablespoons olive oil

1 teaspoon fresh thyme, chopped

1 teaspoon fresh tarragon, chopped

1 tablespoon garlic, pared and chopped

2 to 3 cups chicken stock

Salt and pepper to taste

Two boneless lamb loins

Olive oil as needed

One bunch spinach, cleaned and roughly chopped

4 ounces Chevre cheese

⅓ cup roasted pine nuts

Over medium heat, saute the carrot and onion in the olive oil until softened but not brown. Add the thyme, tarragon, and garlic. Stirring constantly, cook the vegetables for 1 minute more. Stir the lentils into the vegetables. Add the stock and heat to simmer. Cover and cook for 20 minutes or until the lentils are al dente. Season with salt and pepper. Keep covered; reserve.

Brown the lamb loins in oil for 1 to 2 minutes over medium heat. Lower the heat and cook the loins for 1 to 2 minutes more, or until medium-rare.

Blanch the spinach for 10 seconds in boiling water. Strain and quickly stir into the lentil mixture.

To serve: Thinly slice the lamb. Distribute the lentil mixture onto four plates. Decoratively arrange slices of the lamb on top of the lentils. Crumble chevre over each serving of salad and sprinkle pine nuts on top.

Serves 4

Nutritional analysis per serving	910 calories	29.84 g carbohydrate	230.9 mg cholesterol	7.387 g dietary fiber
	72.81 g protein	55.7 g fat	1015 mg sodium	

WILD RICE AND LENTIL SALAD

¼ cup lentils, rinsed

½ cup water

½ cup cooked wild rice

1½ cups cooked chicken

½ cups reduced-calorie mayonnaise

¼ cup lemon juice

One can (8 ounces) water chestnuts, drained

¼ cup milk

1½ teaspoons grated onion

½ teaspoon minced garlic

⅔ cup sunflower seeds

1 tablespoon chopped red pepper

½ cup green grapes

Cook the lentils in the water for 25 minutes or until just tender. Cool. Toss the lentils together with all the remaining ingredients except for the sunflower seeds, red pepper, and grapes. Add these just before serving.

Serves 6

The unique combination of volcanic soil, mellow sunshine, and just enough moisture from snow, rain and dew, make the area in eastern Washington and northern Idaho known as the "Palouse" the ideal microclimate for producing lentils and split peas which are unrivaled anywhere in the world.

Nutritional analysis per serving | 331.9 calories | 21.76 g carbohydrate | 8.042 mg cholesterol | 2.351 g dietary fiber
| 12.5 g protein | 22.72 g fat | 361.5 mg sodium |

Split Pea and Pasta Vegetable Medley

1 cup split peas, rinsed

2 cups chicken broth or water

2 cups corkscrew pasta, cooked and drained

1 cup diced cooked chicken, optional

⅓ cup diced red bell pepper

⅓ cup diced green bell pepper

⅓ cup diced yellow onion

⅓ cup sliced black olives

2 tablespoons chopped fresh parsley

2 tablespoons grated Parmesan cheese

Cook the split peas in the broth or water for about 20 minutes or until tender but still hold their shape. Drain. Mix with the pasta, chicken, diced vegetables, olives, parsley, and Parmesan cheese. Toss gently in a large salad bowl.

With a wire whisk or fork, whip the dressing ingredients together in a small bowl. Pour the dressing over the salad and mix together to coat. Cover and chill for at least 2 hours before serving.

Serves 8

DRESSING

⅓ cup mayonnaise or plain lowfat yogurt

2 tablespoons olive oil

1 clove garlic, minced

1 tablespoon red wine vinegar

½ teaspoon oregano

½ teaspoon basil

¼ teaspoon crushed red pepper flakes

Salt and fresh cracked black pepper to taste

Nutritional analysis per serving	171.3 calories	18.89 g carbohydrate	4.784 mg cholesterol	0 .739 g dietary fiber
	7.243 g protein	7.992 g fat	250.6 mg sodium	

WARM SPLIT PEAS VINAIGRETTE

⅔ cup yellow split peas, rinsed

⅔ cup green split peas, rinsed

4 cups water

One small onion, diced

¾- to 1-pound cooked kielbasa sausage, thinly sliced

2 teaspoons red wine vinegar

DRESSING

½ cup olive oil

2 tablespoons red wine vinegar

⅓ cup chopped fresh parsley

2 tablespoons coarse German hot mustard

½ teaspoon sugar

Coarsely ground black pepper and salt to taste

Cook the split peas in the water for 20 minutes, or until the peas are tender but still hold their shape. Drain the water and return the peas to the pot.

While the peas are cooking, combine the sausage, onion, and 2 teaspoons red wine vinegar in a saute pan. Toss to blend, cover, and steam for about 20 minutes to blend the flavors, stirring occasionally. Drain off the juices. Add to the cooked peas and keep warm.

Combine the dressing ingredients and pour over the pea/sausage mixture, stirring gently to coat the peas. Serve warm or cold as a salad or side dish.

Serves 8

Nutritional analysis per serving   338.1 calories   16.58 g carbohydrate   27.80 mg cholesterol   0.165 g dietary fiber
                                       11.45 g protein   25.67 g fat   513.9 mg sodium

WARM LENTIL SALAD WITH GRILLED SHRIMP AND CHILIES

2 cups Red Chief lentils*

1½ quarts chicken stock

¼ cup olive oil

One large garlic clove, peeled and minced

1½ teaspoons minced fresh ginger

½ cup green bell pepper, chopped

Five hot California fresh green chilies

1 pound peeled fresh shrimp

1 cup chopped fresh tomatoes

¼ cup chopped fresh parsley

¼ cup lime juice

¼ cup olive oil

1 teaspoon cracked black pepper

Place the lentils in a large pot. Pour the chicken stock over the lentils, stirring as you pour. Heat to a boil; reduce to simmer, cover, and check in 5 minutes. *Do not overcook* — Red Chief lentils should be yellow-orange in color and slightly crunchy. Strain off all the liquid. Place the lentils in a large bowl.

Saute the garlic, ginger, green pepper, and chilies in the olive oil until the garlic is golden and the chilies are bright red. Remove the chilies if desired.

Add the shrimp to the hot pan. Saute until the shrimp are pink and firm. Add mixture to the lentils in the bowl. Add the tomatoes, parsley, lime juice, olive oil, and black pepper. Toss gently but thoroughly. Serve warm or at room temperature.

Serves 10

* Regular dry lentils may be substituted for Red Chief lentils, but lengthen the cooking time to 15 minutes.

Nutritional analysis per serving	266.2 calories	18.80 g carbohydrate	79.27 mg cholesterol	4.262 g dietary fiber
	20.19 g protein	12.61 g fat	568.5 mg sodium	

NORTHWEST TURKEY SALAD WITH LENTILS AND TARRAGON

2 cups lentils, rinsed

1½ quarts water or chicken stock

3 cups roasted turkey, diced

½ cup red onion, thinly sliced

1 cup sliced celery

¼ cup chopped fresh parsley

1 tablespoon dried tarragon

½ cup chopped hazelnuts (filberts)

DRESSING

½ cup mayonnaise

½ cup plain yogurt

1 tablespoon Dijon-style mustard

Rinse the lentils. Combine with the water or stock in a large pot and simmer, covered, for 10 to 15 minutes. Do not overcook. Strain off the liquid and place the lentils in a large bowl.

Add the turkey, onion, celery, parsley, tarragon, and hazelnuts to the lentils. Mix gently but thoroughly.

Combine the dressing ingredients and pour over the lentil/turkey mixture. Chill for several hours before serving. Serve in lettuce cups with garlic french bread or brioche rolls.

Serves 8

Nutritional analysis per serving   264.4 calories   24.75 g carbohydrate   43.25 mg cholesterol   5.844 g dietary fiber

26.14 g protein   7.414 g fat   180.4 mg sodium

Catalanian Lentils with Olives and Scallions

2 cups Red Chief lentils*

1½ quarts water

1 cup chopped tomato

½ cup chopped egg

½ cup sliced black olives

¼ cup chopped fresh parsley

⅓ cup diced scallions

DRESSING

2 tablespoons white wine vinegar

¼ cup olive oil

½ teaspoon dry mustard

Simmer the lentils in the water for 5 minutes; check. Red Chief lentils should be yellow-orange in color and slightly crunchy. Do not overcook. Strain off the liquid and place the lentils in a large bowl. Add the tomato, egg, olives, parsley, and scallions; cover and chill.

Combine the dressing ingredients and whip until well blended. Pour over the lentil mixture and toss gently but thoroughly. Serve in lettuce cups or a large bowl as either a salad or side dish.

Serves 6

* Regular dry lentils may be substituted for Red Chief lentils, but lengthen the cooking time to 15 minutes.

There's no need to rinse Red Chief lentils, as their skins have been removed in a special process that cleans them, too. If you should rinse them, you'll notice that a thin coating of starch on each lentil causes them to stick together.

Nutritional analysis per serving	248.7 calories	27.76 g carbohydrate	45.67 mg cholesterol	7.157 g dietary fiber
	12.16 g protein	11.32 g fat	92.78 mg sodium	

LENTIL TABBOULI SALAD

1 cup lentils, rinsed

4 cups water

One bouillon cube

2 cups boiling water

1 cup bulgur

½ cup chopped sweet onion

1 cup chopped fresh parsley

½ cup thinly sliced scallions

DRESSING

Two cloves garlic, minced

1 tablespoon Dijon-style mustard

¼ cup chicken broth

1 tablespoon olive oil

1 teaspoon oregano

½ teaspoon basil

2 tablespoons balsamic vinegar

1 tablespoon cider vinegar

½ teaspoon Tabasco sauce

½ teaspoon Worcestershire sauce

¼ teaspoon cumin

¼ teaspoon salt

Freshly ground black pepper to taste

Cook the lentils in the water and bouillon for 30 minutes. Let stand for 10 minutes; drain. Pour the boiling water over the bulgur; let stand for 10 minutes and drain. Combine the bulgur and lentils with the chopped onion and parsley.

Combine the dressing ingredients and pour over the lentil mixture. Chill. At serving time, add the scallions and mix gently but thoroughly.

Serves 8

Nutritional analysis per serving   158.7 calories   29.54 g carbohydrate   0.049 mg cholesterol   7.012 g dietary fiber
    6.679 g protein   2.279 g fat   247.8 mg sodium

MAIN DISHES

BACON-LENTIL BAKE

1 cup lentils, rinsed

2 cups water

½ cup chopped onion

½ teaspoon salt

One can (16 ounces) tomatoes, cut up

2 tablespoons brown sugar

1 tablespoon chili sauce*

½ teaspoon dry mustard

Two slices bacon, cooked crisp and crumbled

Combine the lentils, onion, and salt with the water in a saucepan. Simmer, covered, for 30 minutes. Stir in the remaining ingredients except for the bacon. Pour into a slow cooker and cook on the low heat setting for 10 hours. Garnish with bacon before serving.

* 2 teaspoons chili powder and ¼ teaspoon garlic powder may be substituted for chili sauce.

Note: You may serve this dish with meat loaf and omit the bacon. If you do, prepare your favorite meat loaf and place on top of the lentil mixture in a slow cooker. Cook on low heat for 10 hours.

Serves 6

The American Institute for Cancer Research recommends "liberal consumption" of foods like lentils and split peas, which are rich in fiber and nutrient value and low in fat and sodium.

Nutritional analysis per serving	122.3 calories	22.48 g carbohydrate	1.777 mg cholesterol	4.130 g dietary fiber
	6.963 g protein	1.288 g fat	396.6 mg sodium	

BAKED LENTILS WITH CHEESE

1½ cups lentils, rinsed

2 cups water

One bay leaf

2 teaspoons salt

¼ teaspoon pepper

¼ teaspoon each:

   Marjoram

   Sage

   Thyme

Two large onions, chopped

Two garlic cloves, minced or pressed

One can (1 pound) tomatoes, with juice

Two large carrots, thinly sliced

One rib celery stalk, thinly sliced

One green pepper, seeded and chopped

2 tablespoons chopped parsley

1½ cups (6 ounces) shredded, sharp cheddar cheese

Put the lentils in a saucepan with the water, bay leaf, salt, pepper, marjoram, sage, thyme, onion, and garlic. Break up the tomatoes and add to the pot with the juice. Cover and simmer for 10 minutes.

Add the carrots and celery. Simmer for another 5 to 15 minutes, until the lentils are tender but still retain their shape.

Transfer the mixture to a casserole. Stir in the green pepper and parsley. Sprinkle the cheese over the top. Bake, uncovered, at 375 degrees, for 5 minutes or until the cheese melts.

Serves 6

Nutritional analysis per serving   321 calories   40.67 g carbohydrate   29.75 mg cholesterol   10.02 g dietary fiber
                                        20.91 g protein   9.847 g fat   1065 mg sodium

CAJUN LENTIL GUMBO

3/4 cup oil

1/2 cup flour

One can (2 pounds) whole tomatoes

1 teaspoon Tabasco, or to taste

1 tablespoon dried basil

One bay leaf

1/2 teaspoon cayenne pepper, or to taste

1/2 teaspoon black pepper

Salt to taste

Two celery stalks, chopped

One large onion, diced

One green pepper, diced

One Polish sausage, diced

One chicken, boiled, with broth

1 cup lentils, rinsed

One package frozen okra, optional

Make a roux by heating the oil and flour over high heat, stirring constantly until the flour is dark brown and smells nutty. Add the tomatoes and spices to the roux.

Saute the celery, onion, and green pepper until soft. Add to the gumbo.

Saute the smoked sausage and pat it dry with a paper towel to remove the excess fat. Add the sausage to the gumbo.

Separate the meat from the bones and skin of the chicken. Add the broth and meat to the gumbo.

Add the lentils and okra, and simmer until the lentils are tender. Serve the gumbo plain or over white rice.

Serves 12

Nutritional analysis per serving | 439.6 calories | 14.41 g carbohydrate | 75.54 mg cholesterol | 2.784 g dietary fiber

31.28 g protein | 28.32 g fat | 752.4 mg sodium

CASPEAN ROAST

½ cup split peas

1 cup water

1 cup diced celery

1 cup raw, chopped cashews

1 cup oatmeal

1 cup water

½ cup chopped onion

2 tablespoons oil

1 tablespoon brewer's yeast, optional

1 tablespoon sweet basil

1 tablespoon soy sauce

Cook the peas in the water until the water absorbs and the peas are quite dry and thick, for 45 to 60 minutes. Combine the peas with the remaining ingredients and mix well. Pour into a greased casserole and bake at 350 degrees for 1 hour.

Serves 6

Lentils and split peas are a rich source of Vitamin A, which helps keep your skin soft and smooth and is necessary to the health of the lining of your body cavities. It is also essential for good eyesight, especially at night.

Nutritional analysis per serving | 276 calories | 26.06 g carbohydrate | 0 mg cholesterol | 2.925 g dietary fiber
9.502 g protein | 16.23 g fat | 179.8 mg sodium

Cajun Lentil Patties with Horseradish Sauce

8 ounces plain yogurt

2 tablespoons bottled horseradish

1½ cups lentils, rinsed

½ cup finely chopped onion

9 tablespoons vegetable oil

1 cup finely chopped green bell pepper

¼ cup finely chopped celery

Black pepper to taste

½ teaspoon freshly ground white pepper

½ teaspoon cayenne

1½ teaspoons salt

½ teaspoon dried thyme, crumbled

Two large egg yolks, beaten lightly

1 cup fine, dry bread crumbs

In a bowl, stir together the yogurt and horseradish, and chill the sauce in a covered bowl.

In a saucepan, cover the lentils with 5 cups of water, bring the water to a boil, and simmer the lentils for 20 to 30 minutes, or until they are barely tender. Drain the lentils in a colander for 5 minutes and puree them in a food processor or blender.

In a skillet, cook the onion in 3 tablespoons of the oil over moderately low heat, stirring, until the onion softens. Add the bell pepper and celery to the onion, and cook, stirring, for 3 minutes. Transfer the vegetables to a large bowl, stir in the lentil puree, black pepper, white pepper, cayenne, salt, thyme, egg yolks, and ⅔ cup of the bread crumbs; combine the mixture well.

Form ¼-cup measures of the lentil mixture into ½-inch-thick patties and dredge the patties in the remaining ⅓ cup of bread crumbs. In each of two large heavy skillets, heat 3 tablespoons of the remaining oil over moderate heat until the oil is hot but not smoking. Fry the patties, turning them carefully, for 5 minutes, and drain. Serve patties with the horseradish sauce.

Makes about 14 patties

Nutritional analysis per serving   173 calories   15.71 g carbohydrate   31.43 mg cholesterol   2.308 g dietary fiber
5.764 g protein   10.15 g fat   318.5 mg sodium

111

CHICKEN-SHRIMP-LENTIL MEDLEY

Two boneless chicken breasts, cut in strips

12 prawns (3½ inches in size)

2 tablespoons low-sodium soy sauce

1 cup white wine

2 cups chicken stock

1½ cups lentils, rinsed

One onion, minced

1 teaspoon cumin

¾ cup brown rice, rinsed

2 teaspoons nutmeg

2 teaspoons No Salt

Two bell peppers, sliced lengthwise (reserve the ends for garnish)

Eight green onions, cut in 3-inch pieces

Two carrots, pared and sliced lengthwise

One can (15¼ ounces) pineapple spears in own juice

One large tomato, skinned and seeded, cut in chunks

Sweet/Sour Sauce

Poach the chicken breasts and prawns in the soy sauce, wine, and chicken stock until the chicken is cooked; remove the chicken and prawns.

Add the lentils, minced onion, cumin, brown rice, nutmeg, and No Salt. Simmer over low heat until the rice is tender, adding water as needed. Remove and press into a 1-quart mold. Refrigerate.

Microwave the peppers, onion, and carrots with ¼ cup of water until the onion is translucent. Drain the pineapple, reserving the juice. Arrange the carrots, bell peppers, green onion, and pineapple spears in a spoke pattern on a large, round platter. Add the molded lentils and rice over the vegetables. Place the chicken strips and prawns on the lentil and rice mound. Top with chopped tomato. Ladle Sweet/Sour Sauce over the chicken, prawns, and lentils.

SWEET/SOUR SAUCE

2 tablespoons cornstarch

¾ cup sugar

Pineapple juice with enough water to make ¾ cup

¾ cup vinegar

1 teaspoon No Salt

Combine all the sauce ingredients in a pan, cover, and cook over low heat until translucent. Add the reserved minced ends of the peppers you used in the main dish.

Serves 8

Lentils cooked in cast iron or aluminum pans will turn dark. For a more pleasing color, cook them in glass or stainless steel cookware.

Nutritional analysis per serving	435 calories	63.61 g carbohydrate	97.12 mg cholesterol	6.444 g dietary fiber
	31 g protein	5.578 g fat	599.2 mg sodium	

CHEESE LENTIL RAREBIT

1 cup lentils, rinsed

2½ cups water

2 tablespoons chopped green pepper

2 tablespoons margarine

1 cup tomato juice or beer, at room temperature

2 cups grated cheddar cheese

One egg, well-beaten

½ teaspoon dry mustard

Salt to taste

Combine the lentils and water in a saucepan and bring to a boil; reduce the heat and simmer, covered, for 30 minutes. Cool.

Cook the green pepper in the margarine until the pepper is tender. Add the tomato juice or beer to the pepper. Add the cheese and stir until the cheese melts. Combine the cooked lentils and egg; add to the mixture. Add the mustard and salt, if needed. Heat, stirring constantly.

Serve very hot on whole wheat toast points. Sprinkle with paprika.

Serves 6

Nutritional analysis per serving   253 calories   15.32 g carbohydrate   75.17 mg cholesterol   3.75 g dietary fiber
16.07 g protein   14.7 g fat   426.9 mg sodium

CHICKEN WITH LENTILS

1 cup lentils, rinsed

4 cups water

2 tablespoons oil

3½ pounds chicken, cut in serving pieces

Two large onions, halved and thinly sliced

Six garlic cloves, thinly sliced

1 pound fresh tomatoes

2 teaspoons ground coriander

2 teaspoons ground cumin

1 teaspoon chili powder

½ teaspoon black pepper

⅛ teaspoon ground cloves

⅛ teaspoon ground cardamom

1 cup plain yogurt, or more for garnish if desired

1 cup milk

2 teaspoons salt

2 pounds fresh spinach leaves

Hot cooked rice

Simmer the lentils in the water for 25 minutes. Rinse in cold water and set aside.

Heat the oil in a large skillet and fry the chicken pieces until they are sealed on all sides. Remove the chicken from the skillet and set aside.

Fry the onion and garlic in the skillet until they begin to soften. Chop the tomatoes coarsely, add to the skillet, and cook for 2 or 3 minutes until they begin to soften. Add the coriander, cumin, chili powder, black pepper, cloves, and cardamom. Stir and cook for 1 minute.

Put the yogurt in a small bowl and slowly stir in the milk until smooth. Add to the skillet along with the reserved chicken pieces and bring to a boil. Add the salt, reduce the heat, cover, and cook for 20 to 30 minutes, or until the chicken is tender. Chop the spinach into large chunks. Add to the skillet and cook for 5 minutes. Add the lentils and cook for 5 more minutes. Serve with hot cooked rice and, if you wish, top with more yogurt.

Serves 8

Nutritional analysis per serving 565.6 calories 24.38 g carbohydrate 188.9 mg cholesterol 6.65 g dietary fiber
71.04 g protein 20.32 g fat 935.4 mg sodium

Easy-Enough-For-Kids-To-Make Casserole

2 cups lentils, rinsed and drained

4 cups water

One package dry taco mix

One package (16 ounces) tortilla chips

One can (6 ounces) black olives, sliced

3 cups cheddar cheese, shredded

Combine the lentils with the water and cook for 20 minutes or until the lentils are tender. Drain, reserving the liquid.

Combine the lentils, taco mix, and ½ cup of the reserved lentil liquid. Simmer for 15 minutes. In a greased 9- by 12-inch pan, layer: half of the tortilla chips, half of the lentil mix, half of the olives, and half of the cheese. Repeat the layers, ending with the cheese. Bake for 30 minutes at 350 degrees. Serve with sour cream, if desired.

Serves 8

If your body is unaccustomed to processing a lot of fiber, it will respond by producing gas if you eat too much high-fiber food at once. Instead, try increasing your fiber intake gradually over a period of several weeks, working up to the recommended 25 to 30 grams a day.

Nutritional analysis per serving	596.5 calories	59.2 g carbonydrate	44.63 mg cholesterol	9.438 g dietary fiber
	23.42 g protein	32.25 g fat	1065 mg sodium	

GRAND PRIZE ZUCCHINI SKILLET

1 cup lentils, rinsed

2 cups water

One onion, chopped

1 tablespoon oil

Two medium zucchini, sliced

Two medium tomatoes, thinly sliced

1 cup shredded cheddar cheese

One medium onion, sliced

½ teaspoon garlic powder

1 tablespoon soy sauce

½ teaspoon salt

¼ teaspoon pepper

Cook the lentils in the water for 30 minutes; drain. Saute the chopped onion in the oil in a large skillet. Add the lentils and zucchini, and saute for 5 minutes. Add the tomatoes and sprinkle on ⅔ cup of the cheese. Arrange the onion slices on top of the cheese and sprinkle with the remaining cheese. Add the seasonings and steam, covered, until the tomatoes are tender.

Serves 5

Nutritional analysis per serving   222.2 calories   20.82 g carbohydrate   23.8 mg cholesterol   5.672 g dietary fiber
13.28 g protein   10.45 g fat   169.9 mg sodium

JUST PLAIN SPLIT PEA CASSEROLE

1 cup yellow split peas

2 cups water

1 cup sliced carrots

One onion, sliced

Six slices canned extra-lean ham (4 percent fat), cut in cubes

One can (30 ounces) stewed tomatoes

Combine the peas with the water and bring to a boil. Boil for 2 minutes; remove the peas from the heat and let stand for 30 minutes. Put the peas in a casserole. Add the carrots, onion, and ham, and pour the tomatoes over it all. Cover and bake for 1½ hours at 375 degrees. Add water if the dish is dry.

Serves 4

Nutritional analysis per serving	244 calories	36.61 g carbohydrate	13.13 mg cholesterol	3.349 g dietary fiber
	20.1 g protein	3.343 g fat	876.7 mg sodium	

LENTIL BURGERS

1 cup lentils, rinsed

2 cups water

1 cup soft, whole wheat bread crumbs

½ cup wheat germ

½ cup finely chopped onion

1¼ teaspoons salt

Two eggs, lightly beaten

Dash hot pepper sauce

3 tablespoons oil

Cook the lentils in the water for 40 minutes, or until soft. Drain. In a medium-sized bowl, mash the lentils slightly. Stir in the bread crumbs, wheat germ, onion, salt, eggs, and hot pepper sauce. Form into 3½-inch patties, using ½ cup of the mixture for each.

Heat the oil in a large skillet. Fry the patties until they are golden brown on both sides, for about 5 minutes. Serve the patties in whole wheat pita bread or on whole wheat hamburger buns, if desired.

Serves 6

Nutritional analysis per serving	155.4 calories	22.52 g carbohydrate	71 mg cholesterol	4.907 g dietary fiber
	4.907 g protein	3.007 g fat	524.8 mg sodium	

LENTIL BURRITOS

1 cup lentils

2 cups water

½ cup finely chopped onion

One garlic clove, minced

½ teaspoon ground cumin

Dash hot pepper sauce

1 cup mild taco sauce

1 cup chopped zucchini

1 cup chopped green or sweet red pepper

4 ounces Monterey Jack cheese, cubed or shredded

Eight flour tortillas

Cook the lentils, water, onion, garlic, cumin, and pepper sauce for 15 to 20 minutes, or until the lentils are barely tender. Drain, if necessary. Toss the lentils with the taco sauce, zucchini, pepper, and cheese.

Spread about ½ cup of the lentil mixture down the center of each tortilla and roll up. Serve the burritos cold, or wrap each in a dampened paper towel and heat in the microwave for 1 to 2 minutes each, or until the burritos are hot through and the cheese begins to melt.

If desired, serve the burritos with diced avocado and sour cream on the side.

Serves 4

Nutritional analysis per serving	764.3 calories	63.02 g carbohydrate	0 mg cholesterol	6.025 g dietary fiber
	42.77 g protein	39.99 g fat	904.5 mg sodium	

LENTIL LASAGNA

1 cup lentils, rinsed

2 cups water

One can (6 ounces) tomato paste

One can (15 ounces) tomato sauce

One package spaghetti sauce mix

1 cup red wine

½ pound lasagna noodles, cooked

2 cups cottage cheese

¾ pound mozzarella cheese, sliced or grated

Cook lentils in the water for 30 minutes. Drain.

Combine the tomato paste, tomato sauce, spaghetti sauce mix, and wine. Simmer over low heat for 20 minutes. Lay half of the noodles in a greased 8- by 12-inch baking dish. Layer the lentils, a third of the sauce, and then the cottage cheese. Lay the remaining noodles on top. Cover with the rest of the sauce, and then top with the mozzarella cheese. Bake for 45 minutes at 350 degrees.

Serves 8

Lentils and split peas are very low in the sugars that cause gas in some people. However, if you find yourself affected, get rid of those sugars by a quick-soak method of bringing the peas or lentils to a boil, cooking for 2 minutes, then pouring off the water. The sugars go down the drain, and the peas or lentils are ready to use according to any recipe instructions.

Nutritional analysis per serving	210.8 calories	19.68 g carbohydrate	27.27 mg cholesterol	3.309 g dietary fiber
	16.02 g protein	6.597 g fat	717.1 mg sodium	

LENTIL-RICE QUICHE

½ cup lentils, rinsed

1 cup water

2 cups cooked white rice, cooled

1 tablespoon margarine, melted

Three eggs

1 cup grated Swiss cheese

½ cup sliced onion

½ cup sliced, fresh mushrooms

½ cup diced green pepper

½ cup fresh broccoli sprigs

2 tablespoons chopped fresh parsley

¾ cup milk

¼ teaspoon salt

⅛ teaspoon pepper

Cook the lentils in the water for 25 to 30 minutes until tender; drain.

In a medium-sized bowl, combine the rice, margarine, and one slightly beaten egg. Pour the mixture into a buttered 9-inch pie plate, pressing against the sides and bottom to form a crust. Sprinkle half of the grated cheese on the bottom of the rice crust. Layer the vegetables and lentils on the cheese. Sprinkle the rest of the cheese over the vegetables, and then sprinkle chopped parsley on top.

Combine the two remaining eggs, and the milk, salt, and pepper in a small bowl, and carefully pour over the quiche filling. Bake for 30 minutes at 400 degrees or until a knife inserted 2 inches from the center comes out clean. (The center should be very moist and not quite set when the quiche is done. It will set up quickly.) Let the quiche stand for 5 minutes before serving.

Makes 6 wedges

Nutritional analysis per serving | 289.8 calories | 34.19 g carbohydrate | 131.9 mg cholesterol | 3.027 g dietary fiber
13.95 g protein | 10.83 g fat | 249.7 mg sodium

LENTIL SPAGHETTI SAUCE

2 tablespoons olive oil (or vegetable oil)

One medium onion, chopped

Four garlic cloves, minced

1 cup fresh mushrooms, sliced

8 ounces tomato sauce

4 ounces tomato paste

2⅓ cups water

½ cup lentils, rinsed

1½ teaspoons crushed basil

1 teaspoon dried oregano

1 teaspoon white sugar

One bay leaf

½ teaspoon salt

⅛ teaspoon pepper

Saute the onion, garlic, and mushrooms in the oil until the onion is soft. Add the remaining ingredients. Bring to a boil. Reduce the heat, cover, and let simmer on low heat for 30 to 40 minutes.

Cook spaghetti according to package directions. Top with sauce.

Serves 6

Carbohydrates and fats are major sources of energy in the diet. But fat consumption means high cholesterol and weight gain. Complex carbohydrates (like split peas and lentils) release energy steadily and slowly, whereas simple carbohydrates (found in refined sugar) are processed too rapidly, leaving the body tired. Nutrition experts recommend that athletes and active people avoid simple carbohydrates and consume complex ones for maximum strength and endurance.

Nutritional analysis per serving	138 calories	20.1 g carbohydrate	0 mg cholesterol	2.89 g dietary fiber
	5.9 g protein	4.9 g fat	443.4 mg sodium	

LENTIL TOSTADAS

1 cup lentils, rinsed

2 cups water

8 ounces tomato sauce

Two garlic cloves, minced

1 tablespoon chili powder

1 teaspoon cumin

½ teaspoon crushed chili pepper

Four flour tortillas

1½ teaspoons oil

4 cups shredded romaine

One tomato, chopped

8 ounces low-fat yogurt

¼ cup sliced green onion

2 tablespoons sliced black olives

In a saucepan, combine the lentils with the water and bring to a boil; cover, reduce the heat, and simmer for 30 minutes. Drain, then add the tomato sauce, garlic, chili powder, cumin, and chili pepper. Cover and simmer for 30 minutes.

Brush both sides of the flour tortillas with the oil. Place the tortillas on a baking sheet and bake in a 400-degree oven for 5 minutes or until crisp. Cover each tortilla with a quarter of the lentil mixture, and the romaine, tomato, yogurt, green onion, and black olives.

Serves 4

Nutritional analysis per serving   369 calories   59 g carbohydrate   0 mg cholesterol   7 g dietary fiber
    21 g protein   12 g fat   436 mg sodium

LENTILS CHILI RELLENOS

1 cup lentils, rinsed

2 cups water

8 ounces Monterey Jack cheese, grated

Two cans (7 ounces) peeled, whole, mild green chilies

Four eggs, separated

½ cup evaporated milk

¼ cup flour

Combine the lentils with the water and simmer, covered, until the lentils are tender, for about 30 minutes. Drain and reserve half of the lentils to use in the sauce. Cool the remaining lentils and combine with the grated cheese.

Layer ingredients in a 12- by 8-inch dish as follows: half of the chilies, the lentil-cheese mixture, and the remaining chilies.

Beat the egg whites until stiff. Beat the egg yolks until lemon-colored; blend in the milk and flour with the yolks until smooth. Fold into the egg whites and pour over the chilies in the casserole dish. Bake for 45 to 60 minutes at 350 degrees until the custard is set and the top is golden brown.

SAUCE

Reserved lentils

1 cup tomato sauce

1 teaspoon oregano

¼ cup chopped onion

One garlic clove

Combine all the sauce ingredients in a blender and blend until smooth. Pour the sauce hot over the casserole. Garnish the dish with 2 cups of chopped, fresh tomatoes and ¼ cup of chopped green onion, and serve.

Serves 8

Nutritional analysis per serving	145.7 calories	21.24 g carbohydrate	0.036 mg cholesterol	5.07 g dietary fiber
	5.779 g protein	4.67 g fat	454.5 mg sodium	

LENTILS MEXICANOS

1 cup lentils, rinsed

2 cups water

1 cup chopped onion

One garlic clove, chopped finely

2 tablespoons vegetable oil

One can sliced black olives, drained and divided

One can (28 ounces) tomatoes, drained, seeded, and coarsely chopped

One can (4 ounces) diced green chilies

1 teaspoon ground cumin

1 teaspoon salt

2 cups grated (8 ounces) Jack cheese

2 tablespoons chopped cilantro (parsley may be substituted)

2 cups plain tortilla chips

Simmer the lentils in the water, covered, until just tender, for about 30 minutes.

Meanwhile, saute the onion and garlic in the oil until the onion is translucent. Reserving 2 tablespoons of the olives, stir in the remaining olives, and the tomatoes, green chilies, cumin, and salt. Combine the lentils and onion mixture.

Spread the mixture in a 9- by 9-inch baking dish. Top with the cheese and then the cilantro. Insert the tortilla chips into the casserole around the edges. Garnish with the reserved olives. Bake in a 350-degree oven until the casserole heats through and the cheese melts — about 15 minutes.

Serves 4 to 6

Nutritional analysis per serving	408 calories	33.63 g carbohydrate	0 mg cholesterol	6.627 g dietary fiber
	20.60 g protein	22.73 g fat	1072 mg sodium	

MEXICAN-STYLE LENTIL PIZZA

⅔ cup lentils, rinsed

2¾ cups water, divided

One onion, chopped

One garlic clove, minced

1 small bay leaf

One dry red chili pepper, crumbled

½ teaspoon salt

⅛ teaspoon pepper

2 tablespoons oil

1 pound ground beef, browned

One package taco seasoning mix

3 tablespoons green chilies, seeded and chopped

One package hot roll mix

2 tablespoons cornmeal

1 cup shredded sharp cheddar cheese

1 cup shredded mozzarella cheese

1 cup shredded lettuce

1 cup chopped tomato

½ cup chopped onion

Taco sauce

Combine the lentils, 1 cup of the water, the onion, garlic, bay leaf, chili pepper, salt, and pepper. Bring to a boil; reduce the heat, cover, and simmer for 40 minutes or until the liquid is gone. Remove bay leaf. Mash; add the oil and blend to a smooth, creamy paste.

Mix the ground beef, remaining water, taco seasoning mix, and chilies together in another pan. Bring to a boil and simmer for 15 minutes.

Meanwhile, prepare the hot roll mix according to the package directions. Let the dough rest for 10 minutes then roll it in a 14-inch circle. Sprinkle a greased pizza pan with the cornmeal. Place the dough in the pizza pan and spread with the lentil mixture; cover with the meat sauce. Bake at 450 degrees for 18 to 20 minutes. Top the pizza with the cheddar and mozzarella cheeses; continue baking for 4 minutes or until the cheese melts.

Serve the pizza with the lettuce, tomato, onion, and taco sauce on the side as toppings to suit individual taste.

Serves 8

Nutritional analysis per serving: 424.8 calories, 3.655 g protein, 26.93 g carbohydrate, 23.11 g fat, 72.34 mg cholesterol, 782 mg sodium, 26.59 g dietary fiber

MIDDLE EASTERN LAMB AND LENTIL GRATIN

1 cup chopped onion

5 tablespoons olive oil, divided

1 pound ground lamb

Two garlic cloves, minced

½ teaspoon cinnamon

2 teaspoons dried mint, crumbled

2 cups chicken stock, or canned chicken broth

1½ cups lentils, rinsed

1 tablespoon tomato paste

½ cup dry red wine

¼ cup finely chopped, fresh parsley leaves

Salt and pepper to taste

1 cup coarse, dry bread crumbs

½ pound feta cheese, crumbled

In a skillet, cook the onion in 3 tablespoons of the oil over moderately low heat, stirring occasionally, until the onion softens. Add the lamb to the onion and cook, stirring occasionally, until the lamb is no longer pink. Add the garlic, cinnamon, and mint, and cook, stirring, for 2 minutes. Add the stock and 2½ cups of water, and bring to a boil. Add the lentils and simmer the mixture, covered, stirring occasionally, for 30 minutes. Add the tomato paste and wine, and simmer, uncovered, for 15 minutes, or until the lentils are tender. Let the mixture cool. Stir in the parsley, salt, and pepper, and transfer the mixture to a buttered 14-inch gratin dish. The mixture may be made two days in advance, cooled to room temperature, and kept covered and chilled.

In a bowl, toss together the bread crumbs, remaining oil, and feta cheese, and sprinkle the mixture evenly over the gratin. Bake the gratin in a preheated 425-degree oven for 10 to 15 minutes, or until it heats through and the top browns lightly.

Serves 6

Nutritional analysis per serving	665.1 calories	37.01 g carbohydrate	107 mg cholesterol	5.575 g dietary fiber
	33.87 g protein	41.26 g fat	907 mg sodium	

PALOUSE ENCHILADAS

1½ cups lentils, rinsed

5 cups water

½ cup diced onion

Two garlic cloves, minced

½ teaspoon cumin

½ teaspoon oregano

½ teaspoon Mrs. Dash seasoning

Salt to taste

12 flour tortillas

5 cups grated Monterey Jack cheese

Combine the lentils and water in a large saucepan. Bring to a boil. Reduce the heat, and add the onion, garlic, cumin, oregano, Mrs. Dash, and salt. Simmer, covered for 30 minutes. Do not drain.

Spoon ½ cup of the lentils onto each tortilla. Add ⅓ cup of the cheese to each, roll up the tortillas, and place in a 9- by 13-inch baking pan. Sprinkle the remaining cheese on top and cover the pan with foil. Bake for 25 minutes at 400 degrees.

Serve topped with sour cream, green onions, tomatoes, olives, and your favorite salsa.

Serves 12

Nutritional analysis per serving 329.5 calories 28.02 g carbohydrate 45 mg cholesterol 2.56 g dietary fiber
18.33 g protein 15.86 g fat 369.3 mg sodium

PIZZA WITH A PLUS

1 cup dried lentils

2 cups water

1 pound bulk sausage

One can (29 ounces) tomato sauce

1 teaspoon oregano

1 teaspoon basil

¾ teaspoon garlic powder

1 cup sliced, fresh mushrooms

3 cups shredded mozzarella

Two pizza crusts (12 inches)

Cook the lentils in the water for 30 minutes. Drain.

In a skillet, brown the sausage, stirring until the meat is separated. Pour off the fat, add the lentils, and mix thoroughly.

In a bowl, combine the tomato sauce and seasonings.

Preheat the oven to 400 degrees. Spread each pizza crust with half of the sauce. Top with the sausage-lentil mixture, mushrooms, and cheese. Bake for 15 to 20 minutes.

PIZZA CRUST

One package yeast

1 cup warm water

1 teaspoon sugar

1 teaspoon salt

2 tablespoons olive oil

3½ cups sifted flour

Dissolve the yeast in the water in a large bowl. Stir in the sugar, salt, and oil. Add 2 cups of the flour and beat until smooth. Add enough of the remaining flour to make a soft dough.

Turn out the dough on a lightly floured board; knead until smooth and elastic. Place the dough in a greased bowl and brush the top with oil. Cover the dough and let it rise in a warm place until it doubles. Punch down the dough and shape at once into two 12-inch pizza crusts. Place on greased pizza pans.

Makes 16 slices

Nutritional analysis per serving   313.6 calories   29.85 g carbohydrate   35.21 mg cholesterol   2.934 g dietary fiber
16.47 g protein   14.28 g fat   943.3 mg sodium

EASY FRIDAY NIGHT SUPPER

Three medium baking potatoes

1 cup lentils, rinsed

2 cups water

1 pound lean ground beef

One small onion, chopped

One can condensed tomato soup

½ teaspoon salt

⅛ teaspoon pepper

Scrub the potatoes and pierce the skins with a fork. Microwave the potatoes on high, uncovered, for 8 to 10 minutes or until nearly tender, rearranging once. Set aside to cool.

Combine the lentils with the water and bring to a boil. Reduce the heat, cover, and simmer for 30 minutes, or until tender. *Do not drain.*

Crumble the beef in a 3-quart microwave dish; add the onion. Microwave uncovered on high for 5 to 6 minutes, or until the beef is set, stirring once or twice. Drain and break the beef into small pieces.

Peel the potatoes and slice thinly. Combine all the ingredients. Cover and microwave on high for 10 to 12 minutes or until hot.

Serves 10

Nutritional analysis per serving	245.6 calories	25.93 g carbohydrate	39.49 mg cholesterol	3.675 g dietary fiber
	16.18 g protein	8.718 g fat	275.5 mg sodium	

POTATO BAKE VEGETARIAN

1¼ cups lentils, rinsed

3 cups water

One bay leaf

One garlic clove, minced

2 teaspoons oil

1 teaspoon salt

2 tablespoons margarine

⅓ cup chopped green pepper

One jar (2 ounces) pimiento, chopped

1 tablespoon paprika

Six medium baking potatoes

1½ cups grated cheddar cheese

Cover the lentils with the water; add the bay leaf, garlic, oil, and salt. Bring the lentils to a boil; reduce the heat and cover. Simmer until the lentils are tender but still hold their shape, for about 25 to 30 minutes. Remove the bay leaf and drain off the excess water.

Add the margarine, green pepper, pimiento, and paprika to the lentils. Cover and allow the green pepper to heat through, and the flavors to mellow.

Bake the potatoes in the microwave, according to microwave directions. Slit the top of each potato crosswise. Press open and put in a pat of margarine, if desired. Top each potato with ⅓ cup of the lentil mixture. Sprinkle with grated cheese.

Serves 6

Nutritional analysis per serving   390.8 calories   63.14 g carbohydrate   19.83 mg cholesterol   7.615 g dietary fiber
                                      14.01 g protein   10.08 g fat   416.7 mg sodium

PRIZE POTLUCK CASSEROLE

1 cup lentils, rinsed and drained

2 cups water

One can (16 ounces) tomatoes

¼ cup minced onion

¼ cup chopped green pepper

1 teaspoon salt

½ teaspoon dry mustard

¼ teaspoon Worcestershire sauce

⅛ teaspoon pepper

⅛ teaspoon thyme

1 pound Polish sausage, cut in 1½-inch slices

Cook the lentils in the water until tender, about 30 minutes. Combine the lentils with the tomatoes, onion, green pepper, and seasonings. Turn into a 9- by 13-inch casserole. Top with the sausage. Cover the casserole and bake for 45 minutes at 350 degrees. Remove the cover and bake for 15 minutes longer.

Serves 6

Nutritional analysis per serving | 336.7 calories | 18.5 g carbohydrate | 52.95 mg cholesterol | 4.08 g dietary fiber

16.92 g protein | 22.02 g fat | 1170 mg sodium

RED LENTIL-VEGETABLE STIR-FRY

1 cup Red Chief lentils

2½ cups water

1 teaspoon vinegar

½ teaspoon salt

2 cups sliced zucchini squash

1 cup sliced, fresh mushrooms

1 cup coarsely chopped onion

Two garlic cloves, minced

½ teaspoon each:

    Crushed basil

    Rosemary leaves

¼ cup butter or margarine

In a 2-quart saucepan, combine the lentils, water, vinegar, and salt. Cover; bring the lentils to a boil. Remove the pan from the heat and let stand for 5 minutes. Rinse the lentils with cold water.

Meanwhile, in a skillet, cook the zucchini, mushrooms, onion, and garlic with the basil and rosemary in butter until the vegetables are tender. Add the lentils. Heat, stirring occasionally. Serve the dish hot or cold.

Serves 6

Nutritional analysis per serving   158 calories   17.36 g carbohydrate   0 mg cholesterol   4.525 g dietary fiber
     6.558 g protein   7.815 g fat   289.3 mg sodium

SPINACH-LENTIL SAUTE

2 cups lentils, rinsed

2 quarts water

1 cup diced onion

2 teaspoons garlic, chopped finely

3 tablespoons olive oil

1 pound fresh mushrooms, quartered

One package (10 ounces) frozen, chopped spinach, thawed

1 teaspoon salt

¼ teaspoon pepper

⅛ teaspoon cayenne

1 cup grated Swiss cheese

Bring the water to a boil and then add the lentils. Simmer until the lentils are tender, about 20 to 25 minutes. Drain.

Saute the onion and garlic in the olive oil until softened, for about 3 to 4 minutes. Stir in the mushrooms, spinach, salt, pepper, and cayenne. Saute the mixture until the mushrooms are almost cooked through. Stir in the lentils and heat through. Remove from the heat to a serving dish and sprinkle with cheese.

Serves 6

Fiber is the part of the food plant that the body cannot digest. That's ok, because fiber serves as a scrub-brush throughout your body. As fiber passes through the stomach and lower intestine, it aids in the removal of fats, cholesterol, residual food material, and potential carcinogens. A daily diet of split peas, lentils, or other legumes is a good way to help the digestive track and establish regular intestinal movement.

Nutritional analysis per serving | 278 calories | 34.55 g carbohydrate | 8.667 mg cholesterol | 9.018 g dietary fiber
| 16.77 g protein | 9.85 g fat | 463.6 mg sodium |

STROGANOFF SAUCE

¾ cups lentils, rinsed

1½ cups water

3 tablespoons margarine

One medium onion, finely chopped

1 cup sliced, fresh mushrooms

2 tablespoons flour

⅔ to 1 cup water

16 ounces sour cream*

1½ teaspoons instant beef bouillon granules

Salt and pepper to taste

Cook the lentils in the water for 30 minutes. Drain.

Saute the onion and mushrooms in the margarine until the onion is soft (for about 3 to 4 minutes). Add the flour and stir. Add the water (to the consistency of pastry). Remove the sauce from the heat and stir in the sour cream. Return to the heat and warm through (do not boil). Add the lentils, bouillon, salt, and pepper; stir.

Cook the sauce over low to medium heat for 10 to 15 minutes. If necessary, thin with additional water. Serve the sauce over cooked noodles or rice.

* For a low-calorie variation, substitute 2 cups of plain yogurt for the sour cream.

Serves 4

Nutritional analysis per serving	429.6 calories	25.09 g carbohydrate	51.05 mg cholesterol	4.338 g dietary fiber
	10.97 g protein	32.9 g fat	509.7 mg sodium	

STUFFED CABBAGE ROLLS WITH MUSTARD SAUCE

2 to 2½ pounds cabbage, cored

½ cup finely chopped onion

2 tablespoons unsalted butter

4 cups chicken stock, or canned chicken broth

½ pound sweet potatoes, peeled and grated coarse

1½ cups lentils, rinsed

½ pound kielbasa or other cooked smoked sausage, cut into ¼-inch pieces

¼ cup white-wine vinegar

⅜ cup prepared mustard

Salt and pepper to taste

¼ tablespoon firmly packed brown sugar

One container (1 pound) plain yogurt

In a kettle of boiling water, boil the cabbage for 15 minutes, or until it softens; transfer the cabbage with slotted spoons to a colander, and remove 12 of the leaves carefully. (If the inner leaves are not tender enough to remove, return the cabbage to the kettle and continue to boil it until the leaves soften.) Drain the leaves and trim any tough ribs.

In a saucepan, cook the onion in the butter over moderately low heat, stirring occasionally, until the onion softens. Add 2 cups of the stock and 2½ cups of water, and bring the liquid to a boil. Add the sweet potatoes and lentils, and simmer the mixture, covered partially, stirring occasionally, for 20 minutes, or until the lentils are just tender; drain the lentil mixture.

While the lentil mixture is cooking, cook the kielbasa in a small skillet over moderately high heat, stirring, for 3 to 5 minutes, or until it browns. Transfer the sausage with a slotted spoon to paper towels to drain. Add the kielbasa to the lentil mixture with 2 tablespoons of the vinegar, 2 tablespoons of the mustard, and the salt and pepper to taste; combine the mixture well.

Arrange ⅓ cup of the mixture along the rib-end of each cabbage leaf and roll up the leaves, tucking in the sides to enclose then completely. In a saucepan, combine the remaining 2 cups of stock with the remaining 2 tablespoons of vinegar and the brown sugar, and bring the sauce to a boil, stirring occasionally. Arrange the cabbage rolls seam-side-down in a baking pan that is just large enough to hold them in one layer, pour the stock mixture over the rolls, and cover them with a buttered sheet of wax paper. Bake the rolls, covered with foil, in a preheated 350-degree oven for 1 hour, or until the cabbage is tender.

While the cabbage rolls are baking, stir together well the yogurt and the remaining ¼ cup of mustard in a bowl. Transfer the cabbage rolls with a slotted spoon to heated plates and spoon the mustard sauce over them.

Serves 6

| Nutritional analysis per serving | 463 calories | 57.78 g carbohydrate | 40.28 mg cholesterol | 14.35 g dietary fiber |
| | 25.65 g protein | 16.89 g fat | 1115 mg sodium | |

SUMMER STUFFED TOMATOES

½ pound lentils, rinsed

2 cups water

½ teaspoon salt

One bay leaf

1 pound bean sprouts

One red bell pepper, chopped

1 cup chopped celery

⅓ cup vegetable oil

3 tablespoons soy sauce

1 tablespoon molasses

¼ cup cider vinegar

¼ teaspoon salt

¼ teaspoon black pepper

Eight large ripe tomatoes

Combine the lentils, water, ½ teaspoon of salt, and bay leaf. Heat to boiling. Reduce the heat and simmer, covered, for 30 minutes. Drain and cool.

Combine the lentils with the bean sprouts, red pepper, celery, oil, soy sauce, molasses, vinegar, salt, and pepper; cover and refrigerate.

Peel the tomatoes. Cut each not quite all the way through to form a six-point star. At serving time, spoon the lentils into the tomatoes. Arrange the stuffed tomatoes on serving plates surrounded with lettuce leaves.

Serves 8

Nutritional analysis per serving	200.8 calories	24.41 g carbohydrate	0 mg cholesterol	5.881 g dietary fiber
	8.597 g protein	9.424 g fat	619.4 mg sodium	

SUNDAY PORK CHOPS

1 cup chopped onion

One garlic clove, minced

2 tablespoons oil

2½ cups water

1½ cups lentils, rinsed

Two medium carrots, chopped

2 tablespoons parsley, snipped

2 teaspoons instant chicken bouillon granules

One bay leaf

Six pork chops (1½ pounds)

Snipped parsley, optional

In a 2-quart saucepan, cook the onion and garlic in the oil until the onion is tender but not browned. Add the water, lentils, carrots, parsley, bouillon granules, and bay leaf; bring to boil. Reduce the heat, cover, and simmer for 30 minutes. Remove the pan from the heat and discard the bay leaf. Spoon the mixture into a 12- by 7½- by 2-inch baking dish; arrange the pork chops on top. Cover and bake in a 350-degree oven for 25 minutes. Uncover and bake for 15 more minutes. Top the pork chops with additional parsley, if desired.

Serves 6

Lentils and split peas are approximately 25% protein by weight — and a cup of cooked peas or lentils gives you 36% of your protein Recommended Daily Allowance (RDA).

Nutritional analysis per serving	451.7 calories	24.37 g carbohydrate	77.05 mg cholesterol	6.165 g dietary fiber
	28.13 g protein	27.02 g fat	381.7 mg sodium	

WHOA BOY CASSEROLE

½ cup lentils, rinsed

1 cup water

1½ pounds ground beef

1 cup diced celery

½ cup chopped onion

½ cup chopped green pepper

One garlic clove, minced

¾ cup tomato paste (6 ounces)

¾ cup water

1 teaspoon salt

1 teaspoon paprika

One can (1 pound) pork and beans, undrained

One can (1 pound) lima beans, undrained

BISCUITS

1½ cups flour

2 teaspoons baking powder

½ teaspoon salt

¼ cup oil

½ cup milk

Combine the lentils and water in a saucepan. Simmer, covered, for 30 minutes. Drain.

Saute the ground beef, celery, onion, green pepper, and garlic until the vegetables are tender; drain. Add the tomato paste, water, salt, and paprika. Reserve 1 cup of the mixture for the biscuits.

Add both kinds of beans and the lentils to the rest of the mixture and simmer while preparing the biscuits.

To make the biscuits, combine the flour, baking powder, and salt. Measure the oil and milk in a cup and add together to the flour mix. Stir until the dough clings together. Roll the dough between waxed paper into a 9- by 12-inch rectangle. Spread the dough with the reserved meat mixture and roll up, starting on the 12-inch side. Cut the roll into 1-inch pieces.

Pour the meat into a 9- by 13-inch dish. Top with the biscuits. Bake for 25 to 30 minutes at 425 degrees.

Serves 12

Nutritional analysis per serving | 359.5 calories | 32.45 g carbohydrate | 53.28 mg cholesterol | 5.887 g dietary fiber
21.81 g protein | 16.19 g fat | 648.8 mg sodium

YELLOW SPLIT PEA CURRY

1 cup chopped onion

2 tablespoons margarine

2 tablespoons oil

1 cup yellow split peas, rinsed

1 tablespoon curry powder

1 teaspoon ground cumin

Two garlic cloves, minced

3 cups water

2 cups eggplant, cut in 1-inch cubes

2 cups cauliflower, cut into florets

½ cup raisins

3 tablespoons fresh lemon juice

1 teaspoon salt

½ cup shredded coconut

¼ cup chopped parsley

½ teaspoon white pepper

Pinch cayenne pepper

4¼ cups cooked rice

In a large, deep skillet, saute the onion in the margarine and oil until the onion is translucent. Stir in the peas, curry powder, cumin, and garlic. Cook for 1 minute. Add the water and bring to a boil; reduce the heat and simmer the curry, covered, for 20 minutes. Carefully stir in the eggplant, cauliflower, and raisins, coating the pieces with the curry. Simmer until the vegetables and peas are tender, for about 10 more minutes. Remove the curry from the heat and let stand for 5 minutes. Stir in the remaining ingredients except for the rice.

Serve the curry on a bed of hot cooked rice, allowing about ½ cup rice for each serving.

Serves 10

Nutritional analysis per serving   259 calories   43.72 g carbohydrate   0 mg cholesterol   3.169 g dietary fiber
6.421 g protein   7.173 g fat   261.6 mg sodium

PILAF OF SPLIT PEAS AND RICE

¼ cup corn or safflower oil

One medium onion, finely chopped

1 teaspoon minced garlic

2 cups long-grain rice, rinsed

2½ cups chicken stock

Juice of one lemon

¾ cup split peas, rinsed

1 teaspoon cinnamon

1 teaspoon ground cumin

Salt and freshly ground pepper to taste

1 teaspoon curry, optional

In a saucepan over moderate heat, heat the oil; add the onion and saute until golden. Add the garlic and rice, and stir until the rice is coated with the oil.

Stir in the stock, lemon juice, split peas, cinnamon, and cumin. Bring the liquid to a boil, reduce the heat and simmer, covered, for 25 minutes or until the liquid is absorbed and the rice is tender. Let stand, covered, for 5 minutes or more; fluff with two forks and serve.

Serves 8

Nutritional analysis per serving	293 calories	48 g carbohydrate	0.313 mg cholesterol	0.815 g dietary fiber
	7.88 g protein	7.807 g fat	246.7 mg sodium	

SPRINGTIME LENTILS AND FETTUCINI

¾ cup lentils, rinsed

1½ cups water

¼ cup olive oil

½ cup diced sweet red pepper

¼ cup sliced stuffed green olives, optional

One or two fat cloves of fresh garlic, crushed

1 tablespoon all-purpose flour

One can (14 ounces) chicken broth (1¾ cups)

Two skinless, boneless chicken breasts (about 1 pound), cooked and diced

½ cup fresh pesto sauce

Cooked fettucini, as needed

Salt and fresh cracked pepper to taste

Simmer the lentils in the water for 12 minutes. Drain and set aside.

In a large skillet or Dutch oven, saute the sweet red pepper, crushed garlic, and green olives in the olive oil until the pepper is soft. Make a thin sauce by whisking the flour into the vegetable mixture. Add the chicken broth and continue to stir with a wire whisk until the mixture is the consistency of a thin sauce. Add the diced chicken and lentils, and stir to blend all the ingredients. Simmer for about 15 minutes, or until heated through. Gently stir in about half of the pesto sauce. (The more you put in, the stronger the flavor.) Cover and hold on low heat until ready to serve.

Cook the fettucini according to the package directions; drain. Serve the lentil/chicken mixture on hot pasta. Pass the fresh cracked pepper.

This entree is also very good mixed together and chilled for use as a salad.

Serves 5 to 6

Nutritional analysis per serving	329.7 calories	11.94 g carbohydrate	74.3 mg cholesterol	2.61 g dietary fiber
	26.23 g protein	16.59 g fat	407.8 mg sodium	

RANCH LENTIL CASSEROLE

2 cups lentils, rinsed

4 cups water

1 pound lean ground beef

1 package dry onion soup mix

1 cup catsup

1 teaspoon prepared mustard

1 teaspoon vinegar

1 cup water

Cook the lentils in the water for 30 minutes. Drain. Brown the beef. Combine the lentils and beef with the remaining ingredients in a baking dish. Bake at 400 degrees for 30 minutes.

This freezes nicely.

Serves 8

Nutritional analysis per serving   294 calories   30.17 g carbohydrate   47.61 mg cholesterol   5.183 g dietary fiber
22.99 g protein   9.58 g fat   826.1 mg sodium

SIDE DISHES

HONEY-BAKED LENTILS

1 package (1 pound) lentils, rinsed

5 cups water

1 teaspoon dry mustard

¼ teaspoon ginger

1 tablespoon soy sauce

½ cup chopped onion

1 cup water

Six slices bacon, cut in 1-inch pieces

½ cup honey

Cook the lentils in the water for 30 minutes; drain. Combine the lentils with the dry mustard, ginger, soy sauce, onion, and the 1 cup of water.

Reserve part of the bacon to use as garnish. Stir the rest of the bacon into the lentil mixture. Put the mixture in a casserole dish. Pour the honey over the lentils and top with the remaining bacon. Cover tightly and bake for 1 hour at 350 degrees, uncovering the casserole for the last few minutes to brown the bacon.

Serves 4

Nutritional analysis per serving   457.8 calories   84.8 g carbohydrate   7.995 mg cholesterol   12.7 g dietary fiber
23.58 g protein   4.789 g fat   486.6 mg sodium

CURRIED RICE AND LENTILS

2 cups lentils, rinsed

4 cups water

½ cup margarine

Two carrots, shredded

6 tablespoons flour

2 cups applesauce

One package onion soup mix

2½ teaspoons curry powder

½ teaspoon ground ginger

2 cups water

¼ cup lemon juice

2 cups cooked rice

Cook the lentils in the water for 30 minutes; drain. Melt the margarine and add the carrots, flour, applesauce, soup mix, curry powder, ginger, and 2 cups of water. Simmer for 30 minutes. Add the lemon juice, lentils, and rice. Heat the dish thoroughly and serve.

Serves 6

For a simple side dish, cook 1 cup of lentils in beef bouillon with a bay leaf, fresh cracked pepper, and a garlic clove for 15 to 20 minutes. Remove the bay leaf, drain, and serve — or cover and refrigerate and eat whenever you want!

Nutritional analysis per serving	479.4 calories	73.09 g carbohydrate	0.333 mg cholesterol	9.915 g dietary fiber
	14.29 g protein	16.05 g fat	814.8 mg sodium	

HEARTY LENTIL-BARLEY DISH

1½ cups tomato juice

¼ cup water

¼ cup barley

¼ cup lentils, rinsed

Two celery stalks, diced

Half medium onion, sliced

¼ cup diced carrot

½ cup diced potato

⅛ teaspoon dried leaf savory

⅛ teaspoon dried leaf chervil

¼ teaspoon dried leaf thyme

½ teaspoon dried leaf tarragon

Simmer the tomato juice, water, barley, and lentils in a medium saucepan for 15 minutes. Add the celery, onion, carrot, potato, and herbs; simmer for 30 minutes or until the lentils and barley are tender.

Serves 2

Nutritional analysis per serving	247.8 calories	54.51 g carbohydrate	0 mg cholesterol	11.07 g dietary fiber
	9.551 g protein	0.668 g fat	689.8 mg sodium	

HERBED LENTILS AND RICE

2⅔ cups chicken or vegetable broth

¾ cup lentils, rinsed

¾ cup chopped onion

½ cup uncooked brown rice

¼ cup dry white wine

½ teaspoon dried basil, crushed

¼ teaspoon salt

¼ teaspoon oregano, crushed

¼ teaspoon thyme, crushed

One small garlic clove, minced, or ⅛ teaspoon garlic powder

⅛ teaspoon pepper

½ cup (2 ounces) shredded Swiss cheese

Eight thin strips (2 ounces) Swiss cheese

Combine all the ingredients except for the strips of Swiss cheese. Turn into an ungreased 1½-quart casserole with a tight lid. Bake, covered, in 350-degree oven for 1½ to 2 hours, or until the lentils and rice are done, stirring twice. Uncover the casserole, and top with the cheese strips. Bake for 2 to 3 minutes more or until the cheese melts.

Serves 4

Remember ... don't soak ... don't soak ... don't soak.

Nutritional analysis per serving   293 calories   31.45 g carbohydrate   26.99 mg cholesterol   5.016 g dietary fiber
    19.12 g protein   9.211 g fat   756.8 mg sodium

HOT CIDER LENTILS

1 cup lentils, rinsed

2 cups water

2 cups apple cider

One cinnamon stick

4 tablespoons butter or margarine

1 teaspoon each:

    Ground cloves

    Nutmeg

    Cinnamon

Two apples, peeled, cored, and sliced

½ cup sliced almonds

½ cup honey

¼ cup brown sugar

½ cup apple cider, if necessary, to moisten

Simmer the lentils in the water for 5 minutes, drain, and rinse. Simmer again in the 2 cups of cider with the cinnamon stick for 10 minutes, or until the lentils are tender.

Meanwhile, melt the butter over medium heat and stir in the spices. Add the apples and almonds, and saute until glazed. Mix together the drained lentils, apple mixture, honey, and brown sugar. Add enough cider to moisten, if necessary. Bake covered at 350 degrees for 30 minutes.

Serves 4 to 6

Nutritional analysis per serving   361 calories   54.39 g carbohydrate   0 mg cholesterol   5.252 g dietary fiber
7.606 g protein   11.33 g fat   90.92 mg sodium

LENTIL-BULGUR PILAF

½ cup lentils, rinsed

2 cups water

3 tablespoons corn or safflower oil

⅔ cup chopped onion

⅔ cup chopped celery

½ teaspoon leaf oregano, crumbled

½ cup bulgur wheat

Combine the lentils and water in a saucepan. Bring to a boil, and then reduce the heat, cover, and simmer for 20 minutes; set aside. Do not drain.

In a 12-inch frying pan, heat the oil, and saute the onion and celery until soft; then, stir in the oregano and bulgur, and cook for 2 minutes. Add the lentils and water, and reduce the heat to simmer. Cover and cook until all the liquid has been absorbed (18 to 20 minutes).

Serves 4 to 5

Split peas and lentils fit into the "very low sodium" category of foods defined by FDA regulations. One cup has just 4 to 5 milligrams of sodium.

Nutritional analysis per serving   186 calories   23.67 g carbohydrate   0 mg cholesterol   5.724 g dietary fiber
   5.105 g protein   8.515 g fat   226.7 mg sodium

LENTIL SCALLOP

1 cup lentils, rinsed

2 cups water

One can cream of celery soup

1 cup sour cream

1 cup bread crumbs

2 tablespoons grated onion

½ teaspoon salt

Slivered almonds

Cook the lentils in the water for 30 minutes; drain. Mix the lentils with the remaining ingredients, except for the almonds, and put into a casserole. Top with slivered almonds. Bake for 30 minutes at 350 degrees.

Serves 5

Nutritional analysis per serving   303.2 calories   36.08 g carbohydrate   28.4 mg cholesterol   4.179 g dietary fiber

12.03 g protein   13.07 g fat   661.6 mg sodium

SAVORY LENTIL GUMBO

1½ cups lentils, rinsed

5 cups water

¾ cup chopped onion

⅔ cup chopped green pepper

2 tablespoons margarine

One jar (4 ounces) pimientos, chopped

One can (14 ounces) diced tomatoes

1 cup tomato juice

¼ teaspoon pepper

¼ cup dry white rice

Combine the lentils and water in a large saucepan. Cook, covered, over medium heat for 30 minutes. Combine all the ingredients except for the rice and simmer, covered, for 15 minutes. Add the rice and simmer for 15 to 20 minutes more, or until the rice is tender.

Makes 8 cups

To add color and zest to your stir-fry, cook Red Chief lentils about 3 minutes, drain, and add to sizzling vegetables.

Nutritional analysis per serving   151.7 calories   25.2 g carbohydrate   0 mg cholesterol   5.034 g dietary fiber
7.49 g protein   3.15 g fat   252.8 mg sodium

Split Pea Gratin

1 cup split peas, rinsed

3 cups water

2 cups (3½ ounces, dry) bow-tie or cut fusilli pasta

Two garlic cloves, minced

3 tablespoons margarine, divided

2 tablespoons fresh lemon juice

1 teaspoon salt

¼ teaspoon pepper

⅓ cup grated Parmesan cheese

⅓ cup chopped parsley

In a covered saucepan, simmer the peas in the water for 25 minutes. Add the pasta and cook covered for 15 minutes longer, stirring frequently until the pasta is tender. Drain. Stir in the garlic, 2 tablespoons of the margarine, lemon juice, salt, and pepper. Place in a shallow baking dish. Combine the Parmesan cheese and parsley, and sprinkle over the pasta mixture. Dot the top with the remaining margarine. Place in a 450-degree oven for about 10 minutes.

Serves 6

Serving suggestions: Serve with crusty, hot french bread and a tossed green salad, or as an accompaniment to meat, fish, or poultry.

Nutritional analysis per serving	290 calories	40 g carbohydrate	3.76 mg cholesterol	2.54 g dietary fiber
	12.52 g protein	9.06 g fat	531.3 mg sodium	

SWEET AND SOUR LENTILS WITH FINE NOODLES

1 cup lentils, rinsed

¼ cup soy sauce or Tamari

¼ cup honey

⅓ cup rice or white vinegar

¾ teaspoon freshly grated ginger

6 ounces Ramen or other raw, fine egg noodles

2 tablespoons dark sesame oil (for a spicier taste, use hot sesame oil; or add a few dashes of hot chili oil or Tabasco along with the sesame oil)

One garlic clove, minced

One large carrot, thinly sliced

Half medium green pepper, finely chopped

Two to three bunches green onion, chopped

Combine the lentils and water. Bring to a boil. Reduce heat, cover, and cook for 20 minutes, or until the lentils are tender but still firm. Drain.

In a small bowl, combine the soy sauce, honey, vinegar, and ginger. Mix well and set the sweet-and-sour sauce aside.

Cook the egg noodles al dente (watch them carefully because they cook very quickly), drain, and set aside.

Heat the sesame oil over medium heat in a large skillet. When it is hot, add the garlic and carrot, and saute over moderately low heat until the carrot is tender-crisp. Add the green pepper and onion, and saute just until the onion wilts a bit.

Add the cooked lentils, and the sweet-and-sour sauce; simmer over low heat for 10 minutes. Add the noodles and simmer just until they are heated through.

Serves 4 to 6

Nutritional analysis per serving	206 calories	34.44 g carbohydrate	8.859 mg cholesterol	4.522 g dietary fiber
	7.936 g protein	4.947 g fat	711.1 mg sodium	

CREOLE-STYLE LENTILS WITH PLANTAIN CHIPS

2 cups *Red Chief lentils*

1½ *quarts water*

½ *pound bacon, sliced crosswise into* ½-*inch strips*

½ *cup diced onion*

¼ *cup diced red bell pepper*

¼ *cup diced green bell pepper*

½ *teaspoon minced garlic*

1½ *teaspoons minced fresh ginger*

DRESSING

2 *tablespoons lemon juice*

2 *tablespoons lime juice*

¼ *cup orange juice*

½ *teaspoon cayenne pepper*

Simmer the lentils for 5 minutes. Do not overcook — the lentils should be yellow-orange in color and slightly crunchy. Drain off the liquid and place the lentils in a large bowl.

Saute the bacon until lightly browned. Add the onion, bell peppers, garlic, and ginger to the hot bacon. Saute until tender but not browned. Add to the lentils, including the drippings.

Blend the dressing ingredients together and pour over the lentil mixture. Toss gently and keep warm. Serve with fried plantain chips.

If plantains are unavailable, this is an excellent side dish for seafood.

Nutritional analysis per serving	224.8 calories	18.15 g carbohydrate	19.19 mg cholesterol	4.186 g dietary fiber
	13.61 g protein	11.33 g fat	388.5 mg sodium	

FRIED PLANTAIN CHIPS

5 green plantains

Heated peanut oil, as needed

Remove the tips from both ends of each plantain. Cut in half crosswise. Run a sharp knife tip lengthwise just through the tough peel on each edge of each plantain. Remove the peel and cut the fruit crosswise into ½-inch slices.

Deep-fry the slices for about 2 minutes or until they begin to brown. Remove with a slotted spoon and drain. Press the slices with the back of a spoon to make a ¼-inch-thick chip. Return the slices to the hot oil and fry until golden. Serve with Creole Lentils on a large platter.

* Plantains are large green banana-like fruits found in the produce section of the supermarket. They are supposed to be hard and green. Plantain chips *have not been included* in the nutritional analysis for Creole-Style Lentils.

Herbed Lentil Puree

2 cups lentils, rinsed

1½ quarts water

1½ teaspoons oregano

½ teaspoon minced shallots

1½ teaspoons minced garlic

½ teaspoon dried oregano

½ teaspoon dried sweet basil

¼ teaspoon dried thyme

½ cup chopped fresh parsley

¼ cup olive oil

1½ teaspoons ground black pepper

Cook the lentils in the water for 25 minutes, or until soft. Drain off the liquid and add the shallots, garlic, oil, and seasonings. Mix well. Puree in a food processor with a metal blade, pulsing the blade. Keep warm until ready to serve.

To serve, pipe around baked or grilled salmon or other meat using a piping bag fitted with a large star tip.

When dried, parsley loses its flavor.

Nutritional analysis per serving	135.5 calories	16.47 g carbohydrate	0.000 mg cholesterol	4.140 g dietary fiber
	6.584 g protein	5.458 g fat	25.65 mg sodium	

TUSCAN-STYLE HERBED LENTILS WITH PANCETTA AND ONIONS

2 cups lentils, rinsed

1½ quarts water

1½ teaspoons dried oregano

½ teaspoon dried thyme

¼ cup olive oil

½ pound Italian pancetta, sliced in ½-inch wide strips*

1 cup red onion, diced

¼ cup chopped fresh parsley

½ teaspoon dried oregano

½ teaspoon dried basil

½ teaspoon cracked black pepper

Combine the lentils, water, oregano, and thyme in a large pot and simmer, covered, for 15 minutes, or until tender. Do not overcook. Drain off the liquid.

Saute the pancetta in the olive oil until lightly browned. Add the onion and saute until tender. Add to the lentils, along with the parsley, oregano, basil, and black pepper. Stir gently but thoroughly. Serve warm.

This dish is especially good served with grilled seafood. It may also be served as a warm salad.

Serves 8

* Pancetta is Italian slab bacon found in the supermarket deli section. It is rather expensive. Substituting lean domestic bacon works very well.

Nutritional analysis per serving 337.4 calories 21.70 g carbohydrate 23.99 mg cholesterol 5.351 g dietary fiber
17.04 g protein 20.90 g fat 486.0 mg sodium

Lentil-Orange Salsa

2 cups lentils, rinsed

1½ quarts water

1½ teaspoons ground cumin

1 cup orange juice

¼ cup lime juice

1 cup diced red onion

¼ cup chopped fresh cilantro

½ cup minced scallions

1 cup chopped fresh tomato
(preferably seeded)

DRESSING

2 tablespoons orange liqueur, or
1 tablespoon thawed orange juice
concentrate

¼ cup olive oil

½ teaspoon dry mustard

½ teaspoon chili powder

Simmer the lentils with the water and cumin for 15 minutes, or until tender. Drain off the liquid. Add the orange juice, lime juice, and onion. Toss gently and chill for several hours. Drain off the liquid.

Gently stir in the cilantro, scallions, and tomatoes. Combine the dressing ingredients and pour over the lentil mixture. Toss gently but thoroughly.

Serve with lamb, pork, duck, or chicken.

Serves 10

Nutritional analysis per serving   154.1 calories   20.76 g carbohydrate   0.000 mg cholesterol   4.475 g dietary fiber
6.980 g protein   5.600 g fat   27.95 mg sodium

162

CARIBBEAN GINGER-RUM LENTILS

2 cups Red Chief lentils

1 quart chicken stock

2¼ cups orange juice, divided

½ cup brown sugar

2 tablespoons peanut oil

½ teaspoon minced fresh ginger, or
¼ teaspoon dry ginger

½ teaspoon minced garlic

¼ cup dark rum

½ teaspoon cracked black pepper

Combine the lentils, chicken stock, and orange juice, stirring as you pour. Simmer for 8 to 10 minutes and check. The lentils should be soft and yellow. Drain off the liquid and place the lentils in a large bowl. Add the brown sugar and ¼ cup of the orange juice to lentils, mixing well.

Saute the garlic and ginger in the peanut oil. Add the rum and black pepper. Ignite the rum and cook until the flames subside. This will burn off the alcohol and leave a superb rum/ginger flavor. Add to the lentil mixture and puree.

Using a piping bag with a large star tip, pipe around slices of meat, fish or poultry.

Serves 8 to 10

Red Chief lentils, bright and coral-colored, have been skinned and cook in just 6 to 8 minutes. These pretty U.S.-grown lentils are especially nice for salads and side dishes. Look for them in health food stores.

Nutritional analysis per serving   223.6 calories   35.82 g carbohydrate   0.444 mg cholesterol   4.450 g dietary fiber
                                    9.695 g protein   3.716 g fat   376.9 mg sodium

SYRIAN LENTILS

½ cup lentils, rinsed

1 quart water

One onion, finely chopped

One green pepper, finely chopped

2 tablespoons olive oil

One small jar chopped pimientos

1 cup peeled, chopped tomatoes

Freshly ground black pepper

Salt to taste

Bring the quart of water to a boil, add the lentils, and simmer for 10 minutes. Drain. Cook the onion and green pepper in the oil until wilted. Add the pimientos and stir; then, add the tomatoes, salt, and pepper to taste. Gently stir in the lentils and cook, uncovered, for about 20 to 25 minutes.

Serves 3 to 4

Nutritional analysis per serving   145 calories   16.98 g carbohydrate   0 mg cholesterol   3.936 g dietary fiber
5.207 g protein   7.17 g fat   19.25 mg sodium

BREADS & DESSERTS

Excellent

PEALENTIFUL SPICE BARS

½ cup split peas, rinsed

½ cup lentils, rinsed

2 cups water

1½ cups granulated sugar

¾ cup oil

Three large eggs

⅓ cup half-and-half

1 teaspoon maple extract

1½ cups flour

1 teaspoon soda

½ teaspoon baking powder

½ teaspoon salt

½ teaspoon allspice

½ teaspoon nutmeg

1 teaspoon cinnamon

½ teaspoon ginger

Bring the water to a boil; add the peas and lentils. Cover and simmer for 45 minutes, or until tender. Puree in a blender or food processor.

Cream the sugar and oil. Add the eggs and half-and-half; beat well. Mix with the puree and maple extract; beat on medium speed for 1 minute. Add all the dry ingredients and beat for 3 minutes more.

Grease and flour a 9- by 13-inch pan and bake in the oven at 350 degrees for 35 to 40 minutes.

Nutritional analysis per serving   333 calories   43.41 g carbohydrate   55.70 mg cholesterol   1.239 g dietary fiber
6.076 g protein   15.90 g fat   196.2 mg sodium

CHOCOLATE LENTIL DROP COOKIES

1½ cups lentil puree*

2 cups granulated sugar

1⅛ cups margarine

Two large eggs

2 teaspoons vanilla extract

3¼ cups all-purpose flour

½ teaspoon salt

½ teaspoon baking powder

½ teaspoon baking soda

⅝ cup cocoa powder

2 cups finely chopped nuts, optional

* To make the puree, simmer ⅔ cup of washed lentils in 1⅓ cups of water in a covered saucepan until tender, for about 45 minutes. Do not drain. Puree the lentils and liquid in a blender or beat with a wire whip. Makes 1½ cups.

In a large bowl, cream together the sugar and margarine with a mixer on medium speed. Add the eggs and mix on low speed until blended. Sift together the flour and all the dry ingredients. Add the dry mixture to the cream mixture a third at a time, blending on low speed. Stir in the nuts, if desired.

Drop by teaspoonfuls onto a greased sheet pan and bake in a preheated oven at 375 degrees. Do not overbake.

Chocolate butter cream frosting is delicious on these cookies.

Makes 5 dozen

Nutritional analysis per serving	100 calories	9.735 g carbohydrate	7.1 mg cholesterol	0.782 g dietary fiber
	1.639 g protein	6.520 g fat	71.8 mg sodium	

DATE-LENTIL BARS

½ cup lentils, rinsed

1½ cups water

⅓ cup margarine

1 cup sugar

Two eggs, beaten

1 cup flour, sifted

1 teaspoon baking powder

½ teaspoon salt

1 cup dates, chopped

1 cup almonds, sliced

Combine the lentils with the water. Bring to a boil and simmer in a covered saucepan for 40 minutes or until soft. Reserve the liquid and puree the lentils in a blender or food processor, adding the reserved liquid if necessary to smooth.

Cream the margarine with the sugar, beat in the eggs, and puree. Sift together the dry ingredients and blend into the creamed mixture. Stir in the dates and almonds.

Spread the dough in a greased 9- by 13-inch pan. Bake at 375 degrees for 25 minutes or until done.

You may serve the bars as is, or frost with a cream cheese frosting if desired.

Makes 20 bars

Nutritional analysis per serving   152 calories   23.79 g carbohydrate   21.3 mg cholesterol   1.956 g dietary fiber
3.345 g protein   5.703 g fat   106.2 mg sodium

GRANNY'S LENTIL HERB BREAD

⅓ cup lentils, rinsed

1 cup water

2 cups warm potato water, or
2 cups warm water plus 4 tablespoons dried potato flakes

2 tablespoons dry yeast

¼ cup vegetable oil

¼ cup sugar

1½ teaspoons salt

One egg

8 cups white flour, approximately

1 cup whole wheat flour

1 teaspoon dried onion flakes

⅛ teaspoon garlic salt

¼ teaspoon sweet basil leaves
(ground)

2 teaspoons Italian seasoning

Combine the lentils with the 1 cup of water, cover, bring to a boil, and boil for 5 minutes. Remove from the heat and let stand for 30 minutes. Drain.

Dissolve the yeast in the warm potato water and add the oil, sugar, and salt. Beat in the egg. Stir in 2 cups of the white flour, the whole wheat flour, and the spices. Beat by hand until smooth. Add the cooked lentils and additional white flour to reach a kneading consistency. Knead the dough until it's smooth and satiny.

Turn the dough into a greased bowl and let it rise until it doubles in bulk (approximately 1 hour). Shape the dough into two loaves and let it rise again, until it nearly doubles (½ hour).

Bake the loaves in greased 9- by 5- by 3-inch loaf pans. Bake at 350 degrees for 30 to 35 minutes. Remove the loaves to a rack and cool.

Makes 2 loaves

Nutritional analysis per serving   227 calories   41.88 g carbohydrate   10.65 mg cholesterol   1.786 g dietary fiber
                                     6.192 g protein   3.376 g fat   180.3 mg sodium

HARVEST COOKIES

¾ cup lentils, rinsed

1½ cups water

Two eggs

½ cup honey

¼ cup margarine

1 teaspoon vanilla

⅓ cup canned pumpkin

1 cup unbleached flour

1 cup whole wheat flour

¾ teaspoon salt

2 teaspoons baking powder

1 teaspoon cinnamon

¼ teaspoon nutmeg

¼ teaspoon ginger

1 cup coarsely chopped walnuts

½ cup raisins

Combine the lentils with the water in a pan and bring to a boil; reduce the heat, cover, and simmer for 30 minutes, or until tender. Drain off the excess liquid.

In a large bowl, beat the eggs and add in the honey and margarine. Cream until smooth. Add the vanilla, pumpkin, and cooked lentils. In a separate bowl, combine the remaining ingredients except the walnuts and raisins. Add the flour mixture and mix well. Add the walnuts and raisins.

Drop the dough onto a greased cookie sheet and bake for 10 minutes at 350 degrees.

Makes 3 dozen cookies

A half-cup of cooked lentils or split peas contains about 4 grams of fiber and about 115 calories.

Nutritional analysis per serving   67.64 calories   11.59 g carbohydrate   11.83 mg cholesterol   0.913 g dietary fiber
   1.973 g protein   2.602 g fat   83.67 mg sodium

HI-PRO MICROWAVE CHOCOLATE CAKE

½ cup split peas

2 cups water

½ cup margarine

1½ cups granulated sugar

½ cup vegetable oil

Two eggs

1 teaspoon vanilla

¼ cup milk

2½ cups flour

1 teaspoon baking soda

¼ cup cocoa

1 teaspoon salt

½ cup chocolate chips

Rinse the peas. Combine with the water and bring to a boil. Reduce the heat and simmer in a covered saucepan for 45 minutes or until soft. Reserve the liquid and puree the peas in a blender or food processor, adding reserved liquid if necessary to smooth.

Microwave the margarine until soft. Blend in the sugar and oil, beating well. Add the eggs, one at a time, beating well after each. Stir in the vanilla, puree, and milk. Sift together the dry ingredients and mix into the creamed mixture. Stir in the chocolate chips.

Generously grease a 12-cup, microwave bundt pan. Spread in the batter. Microwave for 12 minutes on simmer, rotating once. Microwave for 5 to 8 minutes longer on high, or until a toothpick inserted comes out clean.

Serves 12

Nutritional analysis per serving   404 calories   51.87 g carbohydrate   36.19 mg cholesterol   0.704 g dietary fiber
                                     5.626 g protein   20.45 g fat   348.5 mg sodium

LENTIL APPLE CAKE

2 cups mashed, cooked lentils*

¼ cup margarine

Two large eggs

½ cup whole wheat flour

½ cup enriched all-purpose flour

¼ teaspoon salt

1 teaspoon baking soda

¾ cup sugar

1 teaspoon cinnamon

¼ teaspoon nutmeg

¼ teaspoon cloves

2 cups peeled, grated apples

½ cup chopped walnuts

1½ teaspoons vanilla

* To prepare the lentils for this recipe, simmer 1 cup lentils in 2 cups boiling water for 40 minutes in a covered pan. Do not drain. Puree the lentils or beat with a wire whip until they are the consistency of pumpkin. Add liquid if necessary.

Cream the margarine. Add the eggs one at a time, beating well after each addition. Blend in the lentils. In a small mixing bowl, combine the flours (stir before measuring) with the other dry ingredients and stir until well mixed. Add the dry ingredient mixture to the creamed mixture, blending well. Fold in the apples, nuts, and vanilla. Pour into a greased and floured 9- by 13-inch pan. Bake at 350 degrees for 30 to 40 minutes. You may serve this cake as is or top with a cream cheese frosting.

Makes 20 pieces of cake

Pureed peas and lentils add density and moistness to cakes and breads and extra chewiness and moistness to cookies. And children won't have a clue that they're getting the added nutrients.

Nutritional analysis per serving	195 calories	29.48 g carbohydrate	35.5 mg cholesterol	3 g dietary fiber
	6.22 g protein	6.654 g fat	166.3 mg sodium	

LENTIL BROWNIES

Four large eggs

2 cups sugar

1 cup salad oil

2 teaspoons vanilla

1½ cups flour

½ cup plus 2 tablespoons cocoa

1 teaspoon salt

1 cup chocolate chips

½ cup lentils, cooked 40 minutes and drained

1 cup marshmallows

Beat the eggs and sugar. Add in the oil and vanilla. Sift the dry ingredients and add to the sugar and egg mixture. Stir in the chocolate chips, cooked lentils, and marshmallows. Bake in 9- by 13-inch pan at 350 degrees for 35 minutes.

Makes 20 brownies

Nutritional analysis per serving   311 calories   41.84 g carbohydrate   42.6 mg cholesterol   0.959 g dietary fiber
3.875 g protein   15.78 g fat   126.6 mg sodium

LENTIL COFFEE CAKE

½ cup lentils, rinsed

1¼ cups water

¾ cup margarine

1 cup brown sugar

¾ cup granulated sugar

2½ cups flour

1 teaspoon nutmeg

¼ teaspoon ginger

½ teaspoon salt

½ cup chopped nuts

½ teaspoon cinnamon

1 cup buttermilk

Two eggs

½ teaspoon baking powder

½ teaspoon baking soda

Combine the lentils with the water. Bring to a boil, reduce the heat, and simmer in a covered saucepan for 40 minutes or until soft. Reserve the liquid. Puree the lentils in a food processor or blender, adding liquid if necessary to make the puree the consistency of canned pumpkin.

Melt the margarine and blend in the sugars. Mix in the flour, nutmeg, ginger, and salt. Reserve ½ cup of this mixture, adding the chopped nuts and cinnamon to it, and set aside. To the remainder, add the buttermilk, eggs, baking powder, baking soda, and lentil puree. Beat until smooth.

Grease the bottom of a 8- by 12-inch microwave pan. Pour in the batter and sprinkle with the reserved mixture. Microwave at 50 percent power for 10 minutes, rotating the dish once. Microwave on high for 8 to 10 minutes until done, rotating once.

Serves 8

Nutritional analysis per serving | 525 calories | 82.69 g carbohydrate | 54.38 mg cholesterol | 3.037 g dietary fiber
| 10.28 g protein | 18.19 g fat | 416.7 mg sodium |

LENTIL FUDGE PIE

4 tablespoons cocoa

4 tablespoons melted butter

¾ cup white sugar

¾ cup light corn syrup

Three large eggs

1 teaspoon vanilla

¾ cup lentils, cooked 40 minutes and drained

One unbaked pie crust

Combine the cocoa with the butter. Mix the sugar, corn syrup, eggs, and vanilla into the cocoa mixture, blending the mixture for 2 minutes on medium speed.

Fold in the cooked lentils. Pour into an unbaked pie crust.

Bake at 375 degrees for 40 to 50 minutes or until a knife inserted into the pie comes out clean. Cool thoroughly.

Makes one 9-inch pie

Don't soak . . . don't soak . . . don't soak.

Nutritional analysis per serving	395 calories·	66.86 g carbohydrate	127 mg cholesterol	2.45 g dietary fiber
	7.204 g protein	10.11 g fat	153.5 mg sodium	

MICRO-LENTIL GINGERBREAD

½ cup lentils, rinsed

1 cup water

1 cup packed brown sugar

⅔ cup oil

Two eggs

¼ cup molasses

1 teaspoon vanilla

2 cups flour

1 teaspoon salt

1 teaspoon cinnamon

½ teaspoon baking powder

½ teaspoon ginger

½ teaspoon soda

½ teaspoon nutmeg

Graham cracker crumbs

Combine the lentils with the water and cook for 45 minutes or until the lentils are very soft. Do not drain. Puree in a blender or food processor.

Combine the brown sugar and the oil; then, beat in the eggs, one at a time. Blend in the molasses, lentil puree, and vanilla. Add the remaining ingredients, except the graham cracker crumbs, and beat until smooth.

Grease the bottom and sides of a 12-cup plastic, fluted, microwave cake pan. Sprinkle with graham cracker crumbs and shake out the excess. Pour the batter into the pan and spread evenly. Micro-wave on high for 10 to 11 minutes or until the cake's surface springs back when touched lightly, rotating the pan once or twice. Cool the cake for 5 minutes and remove from the pan. Serve with Honey-Orange Sauce.

Makes 12 slices

HONEY-ORANGE SAUCE

¼ cup honey

1 tablespoon cornstarch

1 teaspoon grated orange peel

¾ cup orange juice

2 tablespoons butter

Combine the honey with the cornstarch and blend well. Stir in the orange peel and juice. Add the butter. Microwave on high for 2 to 2½ minutes until the mixture boils and thickens, stirring once or twice. Serve warm.

Nutritional analysis per serving	341.7 calories 4.526 g protein	48.31 g carbohydrate 14.98 g fat	35.5 mg cholesterol 271.3 mg sodium	1.485 g dietary fiber

LENTIL COCONUT PIE

½ cup butter

1 cup brown sugar

½ cup white sugar

Two large eggs, beaten

½ cup lentils, cooked 40 minutes, drained and mashed

1 cup nuts (walnuts, pecans, or almonds)

½ cup coconut (more if desired)

One 8-inch unbaked pie shell

Blend together the butter, brown sugar, white sugar, and eggs. Then add the lentils, nuts, and coconut. Blend well and pour into the pie shell. Bake at 375 degrees for 20 minutes and then 250 degrees for 25 minutes, or until a knife inserted into the cake comes out clean.

Makes one 8-inch pie

Nutritional analysis per serving	558 calories 10.2 g protein	64.26 g carbohydrate 31.54 g fat	112.3 mg cholesterol 219 mg sodium	3 g dietary fiber

LENTIL HERMITS

½ cup lentils

1½ cups water

¾ cup margarine

1½ cups brown sugar

1 tablespoon milk or water

1 teaspoon vanilla

Two eggs

2 cups flour

½ teaspoon baking soda

½ teaspoon baking powder

1 teaspoon cinnamon

½ teaspoon nutmeg

1 cup dates

1 cup raisins

1 cup almonds, sliced

Rinse the lentils and combine with the water. Bring to a boil and simmer for 45 minutes in a covered pan or until soft. Reserve the liquid and puree the lentils in a blender or food processor, adding the reserved liquid if necessary to make smooth.

Cream the margarine, sugar, milk, and vanilla. Add the eggs and puree, and beat.

Sift together the dry ingredients; blend into the creamed mixture. Stir in the dates, raisins, and almonds.

Drop the dough by teaspoon on greased cookie sheets. Bake for 8 to 10 minutes at 350 degrees.

Makes 5 dozen cookies

To have puree on hand, make a large batch of it, then portion it in 1- or 2-cup containers, freeze, and thaw as needed.

Nutritional analysis per serving	84 calories	13.76 g carbohydrate	7.1 mg cholesterol	0.864 g dietary fiber
	1.48 g protein	2.971 g fat	34.51 mg sodium	

Excellent

LENTIL NUT BREAD

PUREE

1 cup lentils, rinsed

3 cups water

Combine the lentils and water in a pan and bring to a boil. Reduce the heat and simmer covered for 45 minutes or until the lentils are soft, stirring occasionally. While hot, put in a blender and puree, adding hot water if needed to get a smooth consistency. Cool the puree.

2 cups puree

¼ cup butter

½ cup shortening

Three eggs

2 teaspoons baking soda

½ teaspoon baking powder

1½ teaspoons nutmeg

2¾ cups sugar

3 cups flour

1 teaspoon salt

1½ teaspoons cinnamon

1 cup chopped nuts

Beat together well the puree, butter, shortening, and eggs. Add the dry ingredients and the nuts. Pour into two well-buttered, 9- by 5-inch loaf pans. Bake at 350 degrees for 60 to 70 minutes. Turn out and cool.

Makes 2 loaves

Nutritional analysis per serving   303 calories   45.87 g carbohydrate   38.15 mg cholesterol   1.902 g dietary fiber
   4.947 g protein   12.05 g fat   236.8 mg sodium

LENTIL OATMEAL CAKE

1⅔ cups boiling water

1 cup quick oats

1 cup white sugar

½ cup margarine, softened

Three eggs

1 cup chocolate chips

¾ cup chopped nuts, optional

1¾ cups flour

1 teaspoon baking soda

1 cup brown sugar

1 teaspoon baking powder

½ teaspoon salt

One small package instant milk chocolate pudding

¼ cup oil

1 cup lentil puree*

1 teaspoon vanilla

In a large bowl, mix the boiling water with the quick oats and let stand for 10 minutes. Stir in the sugar and margarine.

Add the eggs, chocolate chips, and nuts, and mix well. Mix in all the dry ingredients. Blend in the oil, puree, and vanilla and mix well.

Bake in a greased and floured 9- by 13-inch pan at 350 degrees for 1 hour. Insert a toothpick to test if the cake is done.

Serves 15

* See page *xi* for lentil puree instructions.

Nutritional analysis per serving   349 calories   54.09 g carbohydrate   44.47 mg cholesterol   1.258 g dietary fiber
5.433 g protein   13.79 g fat   243.3 mg sodium

LENTIL OATMEAL COOKIES

1½ cups lentil puree*

2 cups brown sugar

1½ cups hard margarine

Two large eggs

2 teaspoons vanilla

3¾ cups all-purpose flour (stir the flour before measuring)

1 teaspoon salt

2 teaspoons baking soda

5 cups quick oats

2 cups chocolate chips (or butter-scotch or peanut butter chips)

1 cup finely chopped walnuts

* To prepare the lentils for this recipe, simmer ⅔ cup lentils in 1½ cups water for 45 minutes in a covered pan. Do not drain. Puree the lentils or beat with a wire whip, adding liquid as necessary to make a pumpkin-like consistency.

Cream together the sugar and margarine with a mixer on medium speed. Add the eggs and mix on low speed until just blended. Add the vanilla and lentil puree, and mix until blended. Mix the flour, salt, and baking soda until blended and add to the creamed mixture in thirds, mixing on low just until blended. Add the oats, chips, and walnuts, and gently blend.

Dip with a teaspoon onto a greased cookie sheet, approximately 1 inch apart and bake in a preheated, 375-degree oven for 12 to 15 minutes. Do not over-bake.

Makes 6 dozen cookies

These cookies freeze and transport well.

Nutritional analysis per serving · 133 calories · 18.21 g carbohydrate · 5.917 mg cholesterol · 0.7 g dietary fiber · 2.323 g protein · 6.044 g fat · 102.2 mg sodium

LENTIL SPROUT BROWN BREAD

2 cups sprouted lentils

½ cup melted shortening

½ cup sugar

1 tablespoon salt

½ cup molasses

Two packages yeast (2 tablespoons)

½ cup warm water

3 cups whole wheat flour

3½ cups warm water

8 to 9 cups flour

For how to make lentil sprouts, please see page *xi*.

Chop the sprouted lentils in a food processor, just enough to cut up the sprouts.

Place the melted shortening in a large bowl; add the sugar, salt, and molasses. Dissolve the yeast in the ½ cup of warm water and add to the shortening mix after it's dissolved and foamy. Add the wheat flour, the 3½ cups of water, the chopped sprouts, and enough white or unbleached flour to keep the dough from sticking to the sides of the bowl. Turn the dough out onto a lightly floured surface and knead until smooth and elastic, for about 8 minutes.

Place the dough in a greased bowl, cover with a towel, and let it rise in a warm place until it doubles. Punch the dough down and let it rise again. Form the dough into four loaves and place in greased loaf pans. Let the loaves rise until light and bake for 35 to 40 minutes at 350 degrees. Remove the loaves from the pans and cool on a rack. Brush the tops with butter if desired.

Nutritional analysis per serving

190.2 calories	35.76 g carbohydrate	0 mg cholesterol	2.501 g dietary fiber
4.883 g protein	3.288 g fat	179.6 mg sodium	

LENTIL-ZUCCHINI BREAD

½ cup lentils, rinsed

1 cup water

Three large eggs

1 cup oil

2 cups sugar

2 cups zucchini, grated

1 tablespoon vanilla

3 cups flour

1 teaspoon salt

1 teaspoon soda

1 teaspoon cinnamon

¼ teaspoon baking powder

½ cups chopped nuts

Combine the lentils and water in a saucepan and simmer for 30 minutes. Drain and cool. Beat the eggs until light and fluffy. Add the oil, sugar, zucchini, and vanilla, and mix lightly. Add the flour, salt, soda, cinnamon, baking powder, lentils, and nuts. Pour into two 8- by 4- by 4-inch greased loaf pans. Bake for 1 hour at 350 degrees or until the center tests done.

Serves 16

Nutritional analysis per serving   337 calories   44.22 g carbohydrate   39.94 mg cholesterol   1.571 g dietary fiber
5.224 g protein   16.19 g fat   206.5 mg sodium

MOIST COCOA-LENTIL CAKE

Excellent

1¼ cups lentil puree*

1½ cups granulated sugar

1 cup oil

Four large eggs

1 teaspoon vanilla

2 cups sifted flour

4 tablespoons cocoa

1½ teaspoons baking soda

½ teaspoon salt

* To make the lentil puree, bring to a boil ⅔ cup of washed lentils in 2 cups of boiling water. Cover and simmer for 40 minutes. Drain, reserving the liquid. Add ¼ cup of the lentil liquid back into the lentils. Puree in a blender or food processor. Yields about 1¾ cups.

Grease and flour a 9- by 12-inch glass pan. Beat the sugar, oil, and eggs together for 2 minutes. Add the lentil puree and vanilla to the creamed mixture. Mix for 1 minute. Sift the dry ingredients, add to the batter, and beat for 2 minutes on high speed.

Pour into a prepared cake pan and bake at 350 degrees for 30 to 35 minutes.

After baking, frost with your favorite frosting.

Serves 12

Nutritional analysis per serving | 369 calories | 43.05 g carbohydrate | 71 mg cholesterol | 1.539 g dietary fiber
5.75 g protein | 20 g fat | 219.3 mg sodium

PEA NUT STREUSEL COFFEE CAKE

2 cups pea puree*

One box yellow cake mix

Three large eggs

⅓ cup shortening

3 tablespoons margarine

⅓ cup sugar

3 teaspoons cinnamon

½ cup chopped nuts

* To make the puree, place 1 cup of washed split peas and 2 cups of water in a saucepan. Cover and bring to a boil. Reduce the heat to simmer and cook for about 1 hour, stirring occasionally to avoid sticking. Whip in a blender or food processor. The consistency of the puree should resemble canned pumpkin.

In a large mixing bowl, mix together the cake mix, eggs, shortening, and puree. Beat for 2 minutes.

For the streusel, cut the margarine into the sugar, cinnamon, and chopped nuts.

Spray a bundt pan and layer ⅓ cup of streusel and then ⅓ of the cake batter. Repeat the process two more times. Bake at 325 degrees for 40 to 45 minutes or until the cake tests done (it should spring back when lightly touched). Leave the cake in the pan to cool for 15 minutes before inverting. Before serving, let it completely cool on a plate.

Serves 8

Nutritional analysis per serving	563 calories	68.84 g carbohydrate	27.63 mg cholesterol	0.756 g dietary fiber
	10.43 g protein	28.6 g fat	429.6 mg sodium	

SPICED CAKE MUFFINS

1 cup green or yellow split peas, rinsed

2 cups water

1¼ cups sugar

⅔ cup oil

3 tablespoons powdered milk

⅓ cup water

Three large eggs

1 teaspoon maple extract

1½ cups flour

1 teaspoon soda

1 teaspoon salt

½ teaspoon baking powder

½ teaspoon allspice

1 teaspoon cinnamon

¼ teaspoon ginger

¼ teaspoon nutmeg

Cook the split peas in the 2 cups of water, simmering 1 hour, or until tender (add water if needed to prevent sticking). After cooking, drain the peas and reserve any excess liquid. Puree the peas in a blender or food processor, adding just enough of the reserved liquid to process, so that the puree is the consistency of pumpkin. Cool.

Cream the sugar and oil for 1 minute. Combine the powdered milk with the ⅓ cup of water and add with the eggs to the creamed mixture, beating for 2 minutes. Add the puree and maple extract, and beat for 1 minute.

Sift the dry ingredients together and add to the mixture, continuing to beat for 3 more minutes. Pour the batter into greased mini muffin cups and bake for 10 minutes at 350 degrees.

Makes 6 dozen mini muffins

Variation: Substitute 1 cup of lentils for the split peas. Cook for 40 to 45 minutes or until soft; then, puree.

Nutritional analysis per serving   49.28 calories   6.501 g carbohydrate   8.906 mg cholesterol   0.065 g dietary fiber
    1.02 g protein   2.262 g fat   47.29 mg sodium

BLENDER SPLIT PEA PIE

1 cup yellow split peas

2½ cups water

1 cup white sugar

½ teaspoon ginger

½ teaspoon salt

1½ teaspoons cinnamon

¼ teaspoon nutmeg

¼ teaspoon cloves

1 teaspoon vanilla extract

Three large eggs

One can (13 ounces) evaporated milk

Two unbaked 8-inch pie crusts

Whipped cream, optional

Simmer the peas with the water for 40 minutes in a covered pan. Do not drain. Puree the cooked peas and water in a blender and then cool. Add the sugar, spices, vanilla, and eggs; blend for 1 minute. Add the canned milk and blend for 30 seconds.

Fill two 8-inch pie crusts with the mixture and bake at 375 degrees for 40 minutes.

You may top the cooked pies with whip cream.

Makes two 8-inch pies

Nutritional analysis per serving   165 calories   27.03 g carbohydrate   63.15 mg cholesterol   0 g dietary fiber
6.582 g protein   4.044 g fat   142.5 mg sodium

YELLOW SPLIT BANANA BREAD

½ cup yellow split peas, rinsed

1 cup water, boiling

⅓ cup shortening

¾ cup brown sugar

Two eggs

1 cup mashed bananas (approximately two or three)

1½ cups flour

1 teaspoon salt

1 teaspoon baking soda

Combine the peas and water. Boil for 5 minutes and then simmer for 15 minutes. The peas should be fairly firm. Drain.

Cream together the shortening and brown sugar. Add the eggs and bananas, and mix well. Add the cooked split peas. Mix and blend in the flour, salt, and baking soda.

Bake in a greased loaf pan at 350 degrees for about 1 hour.

Makes 1 loaf

Nutritional analysis per serving   249 calories   39.81 g carbohydrate   42.6 mg cholesterol   0.871 g dietary fiber
5.036 g protein   8.127 g fat   314.1 mg sodium

INDEX

ORDER FORM

You may order additional copies of *Lentil & Split Pea Cookbook* by writing to:

USA Dry Pea and Lentil Industry
5071 Highway 8 West
Moscow, Idaho 83843

Name _____

Address _____

City, State, Zip _____

_____ copies @ $12.95 each _____

Washington residents add 7.5% sales tax _____

$2.50 shipping and handling _____

TOTAL _____

❑ Payment enclosed.
   Please make checks payable to Washington Dry Pea & Lentil Commission.

❑ Charge to:

Visa # _____ Exp. Date _____

MasterCard # _____ Exp. Date _____

Signature _____

SHIP TO (if different from name and address above):

Name _____

Address _____

City, State, Zip _____